Edward Topham

Letters from Edinburgh Written in the Years 1774 and 1775

Edward Topham

Letters from Edinburgh Written in the Years 1774 and 1775

ISBN/EAN: 9783337405342

Printed in Europe, USA, Canada, Australia, Japan

Cover: Foto ©Suzi / pixelio.de

More available books at **www.hansebooks.com**

LETTERS

FROM

EDINBURGH;

Written in the Years 1774 and 1775:

CONTAINING
SOME OBSERVATIONS
ON THE
Diversions, Customs, Manners, *and* Laws,
OF THE
SCOTCH NATION,
DURING A SIX MONTHS RESIDENCE IN
EDINBURGH.

Non hic centauros, non gorgona, harpyasque
Invenies, Hominem pagina nostra sapit.

LONDON:
Printed for J. DODSLEY in Pall-mall.
M.DCC.LXXVI.

IN REMEMBRANCE

OF THE

MANY CIVILITIES

RECEIVED BY THE AUTHOR,

DURING HIS RESIDENCE IN

EDINBURGH;

THE FOLLOWING PAGES

ARE INSCRIBED TO THE

INHABITANTS OF THAT CITY,

BY

THEIR MOST OBEDIENT,

AND MOST RESPECTFUL

HUMBLE SERVANT.

PREFACE.

THE Public are here prefented with a Collection of Letters, which were not originally intended to be printed, but written in the familiar intercourfe of private friendfhip. Some peculiar circumftances firft fuggefted the idea of their publication. As many as were fufficient for the purpofe were collected together: every perfonal circumftance that might have occurred in them blotted out; and they are now allowed to make their appearance with the permiffion of thofe to whom they were addreffed.

It will probably feem unneceffary, that any farther accounts of Scotland fhould be given, fince two very refpectable characters in the literary world have already communicated their travels to the Public.

But the Author of these Letters begs leave to say, that the following pages do not contain a description of Scotland in general, but of Edinburgh alone: of its Customs, Laws, Entertainments; and in short, of all that relates to the manners of a polished people. They are the living and real sentiments of the Scotch upon various occasions.

Had these Letters contained an account of the Highlands or western islands of Scotland, nothing more could have been said on those subjects, even to the people who admire them most: but there are others who wish to be acquainted, not only with the manners of the vulgar, but those of more refined sentiments, and which can alone be discovered in great cities. It is here where the passions of mankind exert their influence, where objects of power and grandeur excite their ambition, and where the mutual desire of pleasing awakens every faculty. Montesquieu very justly says, " Les etrangers doivent
" toujours

PREFACE. vii

"toujours chercher les grandes villes "comme une espece de patrie." In passing over any country, very little more than the face of that country can be observed. Whatever forms the true character of a people, can only be known from residing amongst them; from being admitted familiarly into their houses; from viewing them in the social and unguarded hours of domestic retirement.

This advantage, and probably the only one, the Author of these Letters possessed, was not small; and should the Public be indulgent enough to think that he has made that use of it he might have done, he will be amply gratified for the little trouble he may have had in collecting them together.

Some apology may probably seem necessary for the repetitions which will be found in some parts of these Letters; and which was unavoidable, as they were addressed to different people, and many of them on the same subject. Where it was in the Author's power to remove these objections, without new-modelling the Letters, he has done it: still, however, many other inaccuracies may occur that have escaped his observation, and for which he requests, with great humility, the candour of the Public. But, whatever may be their opinion, there is one thing the Author is bold to say—That he has indulged no ill-natured or illiberal reflections; but given, to the best of his understanding, the character of the people. Nations, as well as individuals, have their foibles; and though, in justice, he could not help observing them, he has considered them as the necessary shades to improve the picture: and he esteems himself peculiarly happy, that while he offers up this small token of his gratitude for the many agreeable hours he has passed in Scotland, he can pay a just tribute to the merits of the Scotch nation.

CONTENTS.

LETTER   Page

I. *APPROACH to Edinburgh by the Road through Dalkeith.* To the Right honourable Lord —.   1

II. *Situation of Edinburgh, Wynds, and Closes.* To R. D. Esq.   7

III. *On the bad Accommodations for Strangers in Edinburgh.* A Monsieur, Monsieur V. à Paris.   17

IV. *The Description of the Town, &c. &c.* To W. T. Esq.   24

V. *On Salutations on Introduction to Strangers.* To the Honourable W. S—, Esq.   33

VI. *Character*

CONTENTS.

LETTER   Page

VI. *Character of the Scotch in some Points mistaken. Some Observations upon them.* To R. D. Esq. —— 40

VII. *On the Good-breeding of the Scotch; their Language, particular Beauties in it, and Expressions.* To the Honourable William S——, Esq. —— 48

VIII. *On the Executions in Scotland.* To R. D. Esq. —— —— 56

IX. *The Suppers of the Scotch, and their Manner of conducting them.* To the Same. —— —— 64

X. *On the Civility of the Common People.* To the Reverend Dr. ——. 70

XI. *On the Genius of the Natives; their Temper; Persons; Hospitality; Inquisitiveness about Strangers;—The Impossibility of being concealed.—Assisted by the Society of Cadies.* To the Honourable Lord ——. —— —— 81

XII. *An Account of the public and private*

CONTENTS.

LETTER	Page

vate *Diversions of the Inhabitants of Edinburgh; and Manner of educating the young Ladies.* To Miss Elizabeth R——. — 89

XIII. *On the Theatre.* To R. D. Esq. — 100

XIV. *Mr. Digges's Merit in Comedy.* To the Same. — 109

XV. *Mr. Digges's Merit in Tragedy.* To the Same. — 119

XVI. *The Entertainments of Oyster-cellars, and Comely Gardens.* To the Same. 127

XVII. *On the Reception of Dr. Johnson's Tour at Edinburgh.* To the Same. 137

XVIII. *On the Disorder of the Country; the Infrequency of it, &c.—The Sibbins; and Cleanliness of the Inhabitants of Edinburgh.* To the Honourable W. S——, Esq. — 146

XIX. *On the Cookery in Scotland; and some particular Dishes.* To S. W——, Esq. — 154

XX. *The*

CONTENTS.

LETTER   Page

XX. *The Feudal System, and its Consequences.* To R. D. Esq. — 163

XXI. *The different Manufactures of Scotland.* To the Same. — 172

XXII. *The Scotch Bookseller's; their Publications, &c.* To the Same. 179

XXIII. *Some Observations on the Kirk, and Devotion of the People, English Chapel, &c.* To T. M. Esq. 188

XXIV. *On the Dress of the better Sort of the Inhabitants of Edinburgh.* To Miss Sophia D——. — 195

XXV. *On the College of Edinburgh, &c.* To the Reverend Dr. M. at Oxford. — — — 204

XXVI. *On the Lectures of the College; Mode of reading them; and Observations on some of the Professors of the College.* To the Same. — — 211

XXVII. *On Edinburgh as a Place of polite Education; with some Observa-*
                                        tions

CONTENTS.

LETTER | Page

tions on their Trade, and Abilities for it. To the Same. — 218

XXVIII. *On their Gardening, and Improvements in Planting, &c.* To William M—, Esq. — 226

XXIX. *The Superstition of the Scotch; the Effects of it in general.* To R. D. Esq. — — 235

XXX. *On the Ridotto.* To Miss Lucinda B—. — 244

XXXI. *On the Gallantry and Politeness of the Scotch, their Intrigues, &c.* To R. D. Esq. — 252

XXXII. *On the Scotch Dances.* To Mrs. F—r, at Bath. — 262

XXXIII. *The Climate, and its Influence.* To R. D. Esq. — 270

XXXIV. *Funerals, and the Mode of conducting them.* To R. D. Esq. 280

XXXV. On

CONTENTS.

LETTER · Page

XXXV. *On the Laws of Scotland.* To C. C—r, Esq. the Temple, London. — 286

XXXVI. *The Commissary Court, and other inferior Courts.* To the Same. — 299

XXXVII. *The Supreme Courts of Edinburgh.* To the Same — 311

XXXVIII. *On the Scotch Laws relative to Marriage.* To the Same. 318

XXXIX. *Some Peculiarities in the Scotch Laws.* To the Same. — 326

XL. *A View from Rosline Castle.* To R. D. Esq. — 332

XLI. *On the Dancing Masters Balls, and Publics.* To Miss Lucinda B—. — 338

XLII. *On the Assemblies public and private.* To the Same. — 346

CONTENTS.

Letter		Page
XLIII.	*On the Police of Edinburgh.* To R. D. Esq.	355
XLIV.	*On the State of the Agriculture near Edinburgh.* To the Same.	365
XLV.	*On the Scotch Music.* To R. L. T. Esq.	370
XLVI.	*Conclusion.* To R. D. Esq.	380

SOME OBSERVATIONS

ON THE

DIVERSIONS, CUSTOMS, &c.

OF THE

SCOTCH NATION.

LETTER I.

On the Approach to Edinburgh by the Road through Dalkeith.

To the Right honourable Lord ———

Edinburgh, November 5, 1774.

MY DEAR FRIEND,

SINCE you last heard of me, I have been strolling, according to my usual custom, during the Summer months, from place to place, contemplating the beauties of the Tyne-side, (which indeed abounds in beauties of every

every denomination) and from thence I took the opportunity of visiting the most northern parts, which I had never before seen, and which indeed I found more worthy the curiosity of a traveller, than any other part of England.

If I were to describe to you all the beauty, magnificence, and sublimity of Keswick, I should be obliged to dwell so long on it, that, like the celebrated Duns Scotus, I might probably starve before I had finished my page, and inspire you with so great a curiosity of seeing the reality, that a man of your genius and taste for the great and picturesque productions of Nature, who has been an eye-witness to the charms of Italy, would immediately set off, and wonder they had escaped you so long. As I think also, that you must have met with Dr. Brown's comparison between Keswick and Dovedale, it would be needless for me to repeat after him, or relate to you the wonders of that charming lake, which he has painted with all the graces of eloquent language. But there is one thing I cannot help mentioning, which I do not remember came under his observation; the extraordinary echo. As I was somewhat curious, I sailed over the lake, and tried a number of different

different experiments on it; and found in one place, that it repeated the report of a piftol thirty diftinct different times—In fome parts it was a quarter of a minute before the firft echo, and the others followed at certain intervals. The precife time between each echo was always the fame in the fame place, and the report of each echo was equally loud at different times of the day. The Lord of the manor receives a confiderable profit from the black-lead ore that is found in the fand on the banks and edges of the lake, which is dug up in fpadefuls, and after fifting, the ore is picked out of it by the diligence of the labourer. The poor fellow that was employed there, and who was wading up to his middle in water, told me, that he gained a fhilling for his day's work, and often was fo fuccefsful as to dig up a quantity of lead that was worth a guinea. I was fortunate enough to fee the ftorming of an eagle's neft, which was built in the cleft of a rock that has been conftantly employed for that purpofe for many ages, notwithftanding it is deftroyed every year. The man who took it was let down in a bafket by a rope from the fummit of the rock, and combated with a fword the parent eagle, who fought valiantly in defence of her progeny. I purchased one of the young ones, which I hope will be no unacceptable present to your Lordship's menagerie. I beheld also the remarkable Solway moss, which gave me no small astonishment, and as you know I love horrid sights, I could not but wish to have been a spectator of this wonderful phænomenon, which spread itself over a whole country, a deluge of mud; and which,

> ———— Cum flavis messorem induceret arvis
> Agricola, et fragili jam stringeret hordea culmo;
> Jam gravidam late segetem, ab radicibus imis
> Expulsam eruerit.

After passing through Westmoreland, I returned to Newcastle, and from thence proceeded to this place by Kelso, which is not more remarkable for a fine seat of the Duke of Roxborough, than for a romantic and delightful view of the Tweed, which here warbles along his rocky bed, and forms the most beautiful curve, that imagination can fancy; while his deep banks are skirted with trees and brushwood quite to the edges of the water. The country on this side Kelso is naked, vast, and in some places picturesque and pleasing; though its great deficiency of wood is very disadvantageous to its appearance. There are indeed some few gentlemen's seats in view of the road, who are endeavouring to raise plantations of oak, ash, and firs, in straight rows, and sharp angles, after the manner of the English thirty years ago; from which I suppose they are not yet arrived at that true taste and elegance which now distinguishes the parks of our countrymen *: though, at a few miles from this place, I saw at some distance a seat of Lord Abercorn, which seems to be laid out in more modern taste. I passed by Dalkeith, the seat of the Duke of Buccleugh, which I am informed is well worth seeing; but as I shall have many opportunities hereafter of examining every part of it, at present I only surveyed the environs and adjacent country, which has the appearance of richness, fertility, and good agriculture. There seems to be delightful vallies, murmuring rivulets, and a wildness about every land-

* A future Letter will shew how much the author was deceived, and how much he changed his opinion.

scape, which, from the novelty, is agreeable and entertaining to the eye. From Dalkeith to Edinburgh the scene is beautifully diversified. On one side a ridge of cragged mountains, bare indeed, but grand, and of a sublime aspect: on the other, a rich and finely cultivated compagnia extends itself quite to the sea, chequered with farms, villages, trees, and water; whilst the sea-shore is crowned in a serpent form by Leith, Inveresk, and Muselborough. After a short progress on the ascent of a hill

> Largior hic campos æther et lumine vestit
> Purpureo;

and the City of Edinburgh presents itself to the eye, and forms a magnificent picture, with the River Firth, Arthur's Seat, and Salsbury Craigs; the horizon on the other side the Firth being bounded by lofty mountains, whose heads are covered with snow, or concealed amidst the clouds. I reached this place but last night, so that you cannot expect more from me than a general account, with which I am afraid I have exhausted your patience; but you may blame yourself for wishing to hear from

from me so soon.—Be assured, in whatever climate I am found, my good wishes are ever with you, and that I remain

 Your Lordship's most affectionate friend,

  and most obliged, humble servant.

LETTER II.

Situation of Edinburgh, Wynds, and Closes.

To R. D. Esq;

Edinburgh, November 12, 1774.

SIR,

THE many obligations I owe to your acquaintance, and the politeness you shewed me during my stay at Paris, make it impossible for me to deny any request you make. I comply, therefore, with your desire in sending you some account of this City. I know you have read Mr. Pennant's Tour thro' the Highlands; and I can assure you from my own knowledge, you need not wish for better information: it is an accurate and ingenious

genious performance; and, what is the best and truest test of its merit, equally esteemed in this country as in England.

The situation of Edinburgh is probably as extraordinary an one as can well be imagined for a metropolis. The immense hills, on which great part of it is built, tho' they make the views uncommonly magnificent, not only in many places render it impassable for carriages, but very fatiguing for walking. The principal or great street runs along the ridge of a very high hill, which, taking its rise from the palace of Holyrood House, ascends, and not very gradually, for the length of a mile and a quarter, and after opening a spacious area, terminates in the castle. On one side, far as the eye can reach, you view the sea, the port of Leith, its harbour and various vessels, the river of Firth, the immense hills around, some of which ascend above even the Castle; and on the other side you look over a rich and cultivated country, terminated by the dark, abrupt, and barren hills of the Highlands.

You have seen the famous street at Lisle, la Rue royale, leading to the port of Tournay, which is said to be the finest in Europe; but
which

which I can assure you is not to be compared either in length or breadth to the High Street at Edinburgh: and would they be at the expence of removing some buildings which obstruct the view, by being placed in the middle of the street, nothing could be conceived more magnificent. Not content, however, with this, they suffer a weekly market to be held, in which stalls are erected nearly the whole length of it, and make a confusion almost impossible to be conceived. All sorts of iron and copper ware are exposed to sale; here likewise the herb market is held, and the herb women, who are in no country either the most peaceable or the most cleanly beings upon earth, throw about the roots, stalks, &c. of the bad vegetables, to the great nusance of the passengers.

The style of building here is much like the French: the houses, however, in general are higher, as some rise to twelve, and one in particular to thirteen stories in heighth. But to the front of the street nine or ten stories is the common run; it is the back part of the edifice which, by being built on the slope of an hill, sinks to that amazing depth, so as to form

the

the above number. This mode of dwelling, tho' very proper for the turbulent times to which it was adapted, has now loſt its convenience: as they no longer ſtand in need of the defence from the caſtle, they no more find the benefit of being crowded together ſo near it. The common ſtaircaſe which leads to the apartments of the different inhabitants, muſt always be dirty, and is in general very dark and narrow. It has this advantage, however, that as they are all of ſtone, they have little to apprehend from fire, which, in the opinion of ſome, would more than compenſate for every other diſadvantage. In general, however, the higheſt and loweſt tenements are poſſeſſed by the artificers, while the gentry and better ſort of people dwell in fifth and ſixth ſtories.

In London you know ſuch an habitation would not be deemed the moſt eligible, and many a man in ſuch a ſituation would not be ſorry to deſcend a little lower. The ſtyle of building here has given riſe to different ideas: Some years ago a Scotch gentleman, who went to London for the firſt time, took the uppermoſt ſtory of a lodging-houſe, and was very much ſurpriſed to find what he thought the genteeleſt genteeleft place in the whole at the loweft price. His friends who came to fee him, in vain acquainted him with the miftake he had been guilty of; " *He ken'd vary weel*," he faid, " *what gentility was, and when he had lived* " *all his life in a fexth ftory, he was not come to* " *London to live upon the groond*."

From the right of the High-ftreet you pafs over a very long bridge to the New Town. Before this bridge was built you had a very fteep hill to defcend and to afcend, which was found extremely inconvenient. A fubfcription therefore was entered into to build one; and a moft ftupendous work it is indeed: it is thrown over this immenfe valley; and by having no water run under it, you have the whole effect of its height. From it, you have a fine view up and down the vale, and the profpect thro' the middle arch is inconceivably beautiful. Not long ago a part of this bridge gave way, and many people who were upon it funk into the chafm, and were buried in the ruins. Many others, who were likewife upon the bridge, faw the fate of their unfortunate companions, without being able to affift them. All was terror and confternation; every
one

one fled from this scene of death as fast as possible, expecting the bridge to sink under them at every step, and themselves to be crushed to pieces. When the bridge was cleared, and the general consternation had a little subsided, it was found that only a small part had given way; which they are now repairing, and making stronger than ever. But so great was the fear it occasioned amongst all ranks of people, that many of them look upon it with terror even to this day, and make it an objection to residing in the New Town, that they must necessarily pass over it.

The New Town has been built upon one uniform plan, which is the only means of making a city beautiful. Great part of this plan as yet remains to be executed, tho' they proceed as fast as their supplies of money will allow them. The rent of the houses in general amount to 100 l. per annum, or upwards, and are most of them let to the inhabitants by builders, who buy the ground, and make what advantage they can of it. The greatest part of the New Town is built after the manner of the English, and the houses are what they call here, " houses to themselves." Tho' this
mode

mode of living, one would imagine, is much preferable to the former, yet such is the force of prejudice, that there are many people who prefer a little dark confined tenement on a sixth story, to the convenience of a whole house. One old lady fancies she should be lost if she was to get into such an habitation; another, that she should be blown away in going over the new bridge; and a third lives in the old style, because she is sure that these new fashions can come to " nae gude." But different as these sentiments are in regard to living, they are not more different than the buildings themselves. In no town that I ever saw can such a contrast be found betwixt the modern and antient architecture, or any thing that better merits the observation of a stranger.

The pavement of the whole town is excellent: the granite, which long supplied London till Jersey and Guernsey robbed them of those advantages, is dug from the hills close to the town, and brought at very small expence. Maitland, in his history of this town, calls it " grey marble;" but without disputing about the propriety of the name, every one must
allow

allow it the very beſt ſtone poſſible for the purpoſe. They finiſh it with an exactneſs which the London workmen are indifferent about, and which indeed London would not admit of, from the number of weighty carriages that continually go over it.

From the left of the High-ſtreet you paſs down by a number of different allies, or as they call them here, Wynds and Cloſes, to the different parts of the old town. They are many of them ſo very ſteep, that it requires great attention to the feet to prevent falling; but ſo well accuſtomed are the Scotch to that poſition of body required in deſcending theſe declivities, that I have ſeen a Scotch girl run down them with great ſwiftneſs in pattens.

This town has long been reproached with many uncleanly cuſtoms. A gentleman, who lately publiſhed his travels through Spain, ſays, "that Madrid, ſome years ago, might "have vied with Edinburgh in filthineſs." It may probably be ſome pleaſure to this author, and to thoſe who read him, to learn that his remarks are now very erroneous.

But if a ſtranger may be allowed to complain, it would be, that in theſe wynds, which

are

are very numerous, the dirt is sometimes suffered to remain two or three days without removal, and becomes offensive to more senses than one. The magistrates, by imposing fines and other punishments, have long put a stop to the throwing any thing from the windows into the open street: but as these allies are unlighted, narrow, and removed from public view, they still continue these practices with impunity. Many an elegant suit of clothes has been spoiled; many a powdered, well-dressed maccaroni sent home for the evening: and to conclude this period in Dr. Johnson's own simple words, " Many a full-flowing perriwig " moistened into flaccidity *."

Such particulars, however, as these scarce merit observation: they are circumstances resulting from the peculiar inconveniency of the buildings, and not from the natural disposition of the Scotch, who love cleanliness and practise it. They lament the impropriety of these customs, and join in the laugh at the accidents they occasion.

It has been the misfortune of almost every nation to be prejudged at a distance, or to be

---

* Vide Idler.

visited

visited by a number of men whose resolutions are too strong for conviction. They come with a fixed idea, that the Scotch are a dirty people: they probably meet with some person who is so, and would be so in any country, and away they hurry back, and give, as they think, the just character of the whole nation. It has been the peculiar fortune of the Scotch to have been thus treated: but they are a sensible and ingenious people, and look upon these hasty censures in the manner they deserve. But to you, who are " Nullius ad-" dictus jurare in verba magistri," and who are bigotted to no particular customs, I make no scruple of declaring, that this metropolis is not, as some of our countrymen please to say, dirty and disagreeable; but adorned with many elegant and beautiful structures, the seat of several of the most ingenious men in Europe, and who are an honour to the age they live in, abounding in many of the politer embellishments of life, and well deserving the attention of a traveller.

I have the honour to be, &c.

LETTER

LETTER III.

On the bad Accommodations for Strangers in Edinburgh.

A Monſieur, Monſieur V. à Paris.

Edinburgh, November 15, 1774.

DEAR SIR,

SINCE my laſt, which I delivered to your ſon, when I had the pleaſure of ſeeing him in London, I have been a great traveller; and am now ſet down in Edinburgh for the winter ſeaſon. I muſt confeſs I already ſhudder at the thoughts of this northern climate, and look with ſome apprehenſions on the approach of cold weather; the ſeverity of which, I doubt, the feebleneſs of my conſtitution will with difficulty be able to combat. However, I am in a tolerable comfortable habitation at preſent, and have fortunately procured an apartment ſomewhat elevated indeed, but commodious, and in a good ſituation. In a city ſo large as Edinburgh, the ſize of which you may eaſily conjecture from its being the

metropolis

metropolis of Scotland, I make no manner of doubt but you muſt be ſurpriſed to hear me conſider myſelf as fortunate, in having found out a lodging, where I can ſleep without moleſtation, and where I am neither poiſoned by ſtench, or ſuffocated for want of air. A perſon like you, who has always been accuſtomed to meet with downy pillows, and ſplendid apartments, in the hotels of Paris and Lyons, can ſcarcely form in imagination the diſtreſs of a miſerable ſtranger on his firſt entrance into this city: as there is no inn that is better than an alehouſe, nor any accommodation that is decent, cleanly, or fit to receive a gentleman. On my firſt arrival, my companion and ſelf, after the fatigue of a long day's journey, were landed at one of theſe ſtable-keepers (for they have modeſty enough to give themſelves no higher denomination) in a part of the town which is called the Pleaſance; and on entering the houſe, we were conducted by a poor devil of a girl without ſhoes or ſtockings, and with only a ſingle linſey-woolſey petticoat, which juſt reached half-way to her ankles, into a room where about twenty Scotch drovers had been regaling themſelves with whiſky and potatoes.

tatoes. You may guess our amazement, when we were informed, ' that this was the best inn in ' the metropolis—that we could have no beds, ' unless we had an inclination to sleep together, ' and in the same room with the company ' which a stage-coach had that moment dis- ' charged.' Well, said I to my friend (for you must know that I have more patience on these occasions than wit on any other) there is nothing like seeing men and manners, perhaps we may be able to repose ourselves at some coffee-house. Accordingly, on inquiry, we discovered that there was a good dame by the Cross, who acted in the double capacity of pouring out coffee, or letting lodgings to strangers, as we were. She was easily to be found out; and with all the conciliating complaisance of a Maîtresse d'Hotel, conducted us to our destined apartments; which were indeed six stories high, but so infernal to appearance, that you would have thought yourself in the regions of Erebus.

The truth of this, I will venture say, you will make no scruple to believe, when I tell you, that in the whole we had only two windows, which looked into an alley five foot wide,

wide, where the houses were at least ten stories high, and the alley itself was so sombre in the brightest sunshine, that it was impossible to see any object distinctly. And now I am in the story-telling humour, I cannot omit giving you an account of an adventure which happened here very lately to a friend of mine; as it tallies in some measure with what I have already related, and serves to confirm the wretchedness of accommodation which must be put up with in this city. A gentleman from London, who had been appointed to some duty in a public office, came to Edinburgh, and having no friends to furnish him with a bed, and few acquaintance to give him any assistance, found himself obliged to conceal himself in one of these dark abodes, in order to be nigh the center of the town, where his employment compelled him to pass most part of the day. As he perceived his lodgings as good as his neighbours, it induced him to continue there, until he discovered himself extremely weak and emaciated, occasioned by constant violent perspirations in which he waked every morning. The observations, which some of his associates made on the alteration of his *embonpoint*, and

the

the situation to which he was reduced (for from a stout and lusty man, he was now become a mere shadow) persuaded him to think himself really ill and in a consumption. Accordingly he sent for the professor, and another or two of the learned fraternity; who, with all the significancy of pompous physic, pronounced him to be in a very declining state, and administered every restorative which the Esculapian art could suggest or supply. But all without effect: he still continued to grow worse; and at length, almost totally exhausted, and giving himself a prey to despair, he sent up for his landlady to be a witness to his will; who, much concerned for the melancholy event, and with tears in her eyes, said, " How unfortu-
" nate she had been since she kept house; that
" her two former lodgers had died with her;
" that she was sure she did every thing to
" serve them all; that, for her part, she always
" took care that their linen was well aired;
" and as for her rooms, nothing could be
" drier or more free from dampness; that her
" neighbour, good man, was a baker, and his
" oven was directly under them; that she was
" sure, therefore, they must be warm, and it
" was

" was impoſſible to catch cold in her houſe."
— " Good God," cried the gentleman, " an
" oven under my room! no wonder I am in
" a conſumption after having been baked for
" theſe three months." Upon which he ſent
for the baker, and found what ſhe ſaid was
really true; that the oven was immediately
under his bed, and that the decreaſe of his
health had been in proportion to the increaſe
of the baker's buſineſs. The diſcovery therefore being a much better medicine than any
the profeſſors could preſcribe, he quitted this
enfer, by degrees recovered his ſtrength and
conſtitution, and lives now to ridicule the oddity of the accident. After all this, I am ſure
you will agree with me, that 'tis extremely
ſtrange, that a city, which is a thoroughfare
into all Scotland, and now little inferior in
politeneſs to London in many reſpects, ſhould
not be better furniſhed with conveniencies for
ſtrangers, or have a public lodging-houſe where
you can find tolerable entertainment. But it
really has not: and I am the more ſurpriſed
at it; as, in their manner of living, and many
cuſtoms, I think the inhabitants much re-
ſemble the French. But in this particular

what

what a difference between this place and Paris! where in a minute you may be provided with a house equal to one of the greatest nobility, with servants, equipage, and all the luxuries of elegance and taste; whilst at Edinburgh, without an inn to put your head into, and without a lodging that you can breathe in, you are obliged to bless your stars to get any place to repose yourself, till better fortune, or better acquaintance, have interest enough to procure it you in some private house.—It is a pity — it is a disgrace to the country; and I should hope, ere long, the pride or good sense of Scotland will so far prevail, as to establish an Hotel in some suitable part of the town, to obviate the inconvenience of the want of these necessaries. For an example and pattern she need go no further than the metropolis of her sister-kingdom; where Mr. Lowe's endeavours to merit the applause of the public have been crowned with universal approbation. But I am trespassing on your time. How much I am obliged to you for your letter, I am informed enough by Mr. Le M—e, but more by my own feelings. And as I am assured that you are more pleased to oblige your friends, than to receive their thanks, I will only say, that mine are very sensible; and that no man is with more reason, and with more sincerity, than I am,

  Your ever affectionate friend,

    and obedient humble servant.

LETTER IV.

The Description of the Town, &c. &c.

To W. T. Esq.

Edinburgh, November 20, 1774.

DEAR SIR,

YOUR sentiments on the taste of the present time in architecture and ornamental buildings, perfectly correspond with mine; and I agree with you, that we have made a greater progress towards excellence, in a few years, in this, than we have done in other arts, that perhaps are of greater utility to mankind. For the one I can easily account; namely,

namely, from our close imitation of the antique; from our adopting certain forms, figures, dimensions, and colours, which the politest people that ever existed, esteemed the most, when they had arrived at the utmost summit of civilization and luxury. The present mode of colouring ceilings and rooms can never be too much admired: and the paleness of the tints gives to their appearance much grace, ease, and modesty, blended with a certain degree of grandeur and dignity, which seem to take no pains to shew themselves. For this, as for many other good things, London is indebted to a native of Scotland. Messrs. Adams, if I am not mistaken, were the first who introduced this manner; when the Adelphi, which will present a pattern of architecture to ages to come, disclosed the genius of those great masters. But you ask me if this improvement has advanced so far North as this country. I wish I could answer you in the affirmative. I see nothing of it, either in their new buildings, or in their ornaments. The situation of the Old Town renders it hardly worth while making any alteration in the style of furniture, or finishing apartments;

every

every house having the appearance of a lodging. You will be sensible of this, if I give you a short description of the old city of Edinburgh, which I hope will afford you some entertainment; as I know you are a perfect stranger to it. The principal street of Edinburgh is situated on the ridge or *dorsum* of a hill, which rises gradually, and abruptly terminates in a vast pile of rocks, on which the Castle is built, in 55 degrees north latitude, and in 3 degrees of west longitude. At the foot of it is Holyroodhouse, the elevation of which, from the high-water mark at Leith, is 94 feet, and from thence to the Castle 180: that the elevation of the whole hill is 274 feet. The other principal streets are parallel to this, on the south side, at the bottom of the hill, and are called the Cowgate and Grassmarket. Tradition says, the Cowgate, two hundred years ago, was the polite part of the town; and in it were the houses of the Nobility, and the Senators of the College of Justice; but, at present, the buildings are much inferior to those on the top of the hill. The original town has been fortified, is surrounded by a wall, and has nine ports. The buildings are all

all of them of stone of a brown cast, and those in the high street extremely elevated, especially behind, where some of them are ten or twelve stories; and one, I think, is said to be thirteen, as they all formerly were, before a conflagration, which happened A. D. 1690. The reason the buildings are so much higher behind than towards the street, is on account that they are situated on the edge of the hill, in order that the street might be wider, and take up the whole of the ridge, which is about thirty yards across. These buildings are divided by extremely thick partition walls, into large houses, which are here called lands, and each story of a land is called a house. Every land has a common stair-case, in the same manner as the inns of court in London, and houses in Paris; from whence, it is most probable, this custom was taken. As each house is occupied by a family, a land, being so large, contains many families; that I make no manner of doubt but that the High Street in Edinburgh is inhabited by a greater number of persons than any street in Europe. The ground-floors and cellars are in general made use of for shops by the tradesmen; who here style themselves

Merchants,

Merchants, as in France; and the higher houses are possessed by the genteeler people. The merchants here also, as in France, have the horrid custom of painting on the outside of their houses, the figure of the commodity which is to be sold within; which, in this place, makes the oddest appearance you can conceive; for each story, perhaps, from top to bottom, is checquered with ten thousand different forms and colours; that the whole resembles the stall of a fair, presenting, at one view, the goods of a variety of shops. They are likewise remarkably fond of glaring colours; as red, yellow, and blue, on which the figures are painted in black. You would laugh to see a black quartern loaf directly over a black full-trimmed perriwig of a professor, with a Cheshire cheese, and a rich firkin of butter, displayed in black greasiness under stays, petticoats, and child-bed linen. The principal edifices in Edinburgh are the Castle, Holyroodhouse, the Infirmary, and Heriot's Hospital. The Castle, I find, was erected by Edwin King of Northumberland, A. D. 626, who gave it the name of Edwin's Burgh, or Edwin's Castle; and is mentioned by Simeon of Durham,

ham, in his book, intitled, *De Geft. Regum Ang. ad annum* 854. It is situated in the northern part of Mid Lothian, two miles south of the Firth of Forth, and is fortified in an extreme strong manner, three sides of the rock on which it is founded being perpendicular. Within the walls is an armoury and barracks for soldiers; and a very large garrison is generally quartered there. But before I proceed any further, I must entreat you to take a view of the prospect from the top of the Castle, which, perhaps, is the most picturesque and beautiful of any that can be found in Europe. If there is any deficiency in the whole, it is the want of a forest, or some large tract of wooded country; for, in all other respects, nothing was ever formed more pleasing to the eye.

The Palace of Holyroodhouse is a stone building, of one square, surrounded by a piazza. The front of it consists of two towers, joined by a low building or gallery, in the middle of which is a portico, that supports a cupola in form of a crown.

In the gallery on the north side of the square, are the portraits of all the Scotch Kings: the rest of the house is divided into the

Great

Great Council-chamber, and apartments for the Nobility, like Somerset house in London.

Holyroodhouse was originally a monastery, called *Sanctæ Crucis*, and founded by David I. It was destroyed by the English about the middle of the sixteenth century, and nothing left but the church, to which James V. A. D. 1528, added a palace, which Charles II. 1674, augmented. It is a heavy ugly fabric, and has so little the appearance of a palace, that you may well apply to it, what the Cavaliero Bernini said of the Louvre, that it is *Una gran piccola cosa*. It has a park walled in, three miles in circumference, and consisting of two hills; one rising into three tops, the highest of which is called Arthur's Seat; and Salsbury Craigs, a semicircular body of rocks, resembling a ruinous amphitheatre.

Arthur's Seat is interpreted Ard-na-said, or the Height of Arrows, from its being adapted to that sport. The view from it, though more extensive, is not so pleasing as that from the Castle, on account of its great height. The hill on which the Old Town is situated, with the Castle at its extremity, appears from it, like the back and head of some animal,

animal, whilst the steeples, spires, and chimnies bristle on it,

"Like quills upon the fretful porcupine."

Heriot's Hospital is a large and magnificent edifice, and has infinitely more the look of a palace than Holyroodhouse. It was founded by one George Heriot, a merchant in Edinburgh, and was begun to be built A. D. 1628; but stopt during the troubles in Great Britain, and was nearly finished A. D. 1650, when it was taken possession of by the English army under the command of Oliver Cromwell, who converted it into an infirmary for the use of his men, and in whose possession it remained till A. D. 1658, when it was restored to the governors, who prepared it for the reception of children who are fatherless, freemen's sons of the City of Edinburgh. It now contains a hundred and fifty boys, who are under the care of a treasurer, and proper masters to prepare them for business, or qualify them to be sent bursers to the College, with an annual stipend of five pounds a-year. This building cost twenty-seven thousand pounds, and the sum left by the founder

founder forty-three thoufand fix hundred pounds.

Thus, in as few words as poffible, I have endeavoured to give you a faint idea of the Old City of Edinburgh, and I have added thofe buildings which I thought beft worth your knowledge. As it is one of the moft populous places of its fize in the known world, you may conjecture how crowded it muft be, and how little room for elegance and a fuperfluity of luxurious ornaments. But the New Town is in a very different ftyle of architecture: the account of which I fhall referve till another opportunity; and in the mean time, if you blame me for ingroffing fo much of your time, you muft lay the whole fault on your own letter; or rather on my not having heard of you before for fo long a time, " and that ftrong propenfity of my nature to re-affume my old correfpondence, juft as a man does an old love, which lies ftill deep at heart, however diverted or difcontinued."

Believe me, with great truth,
 your moft affectionate friend,
  and obliged, humble fervant.

LETTER

LETTER V.

On Salutations on Introduction to Strangers.

To the Honourable W. S———, Esq;

Edinburgh, November 26, 1774.

DEAR SIR,

AMONGST the number of ancient customs which have been handed down to us from past ages, and which are frequently to be met with on the Continent, the Scotch have one, which has been long out of fashion in England, though it formerly existed there; that of salutation on introduction to strangers. That this was a custom of the Romans, is evident from a variety of authors, particularly from Ovid, who speaks of it in his usual rapturous manner; " Gratatusque darem " cum dulcibus oscula verbis." It is at present common among the Venetians, and practised in many parts of France. That it was usual among the English, appears from many passages of the history of England; and that it was once more so than on the Continent, is plain

plain from some lines of the celebrated Erasmus, in an epistle to Faustus Adrelinus, the Poet laureat: where this great philosopher, in an amorous mood, invites his friend, in the following strain, to repair immediately to Great-Britain, for the sake of conversing with the female inhabitants of the country; " Sunt
" hîc nymphæ divinis vultibus, blandæ, fa-
" ciles, et quas tu tuis Camœnis facile ante-
" ponas. Est præterea mos nunquam satis
" laudatus: sive quo venias, omnium oscu-
" lis exciperis, sive discedas aliquo, osculis
" dimitteris; redis, redduntur suavia; venitur
" ad te, propinantur suavia; disceditur abs
" te, dividuntur basia; occurritur alibi, basi-
" atur affatim; denique quocunque te mo-
" veas, suaviorum plena sunt omnia." The warmth and energy of his expression I should think was a plain proof, that the custom was not only agreeable, but new; which gives me much surprise, since Montaigne and other French writers mention it as having always been the mode of introduction in their country; which if it had, it could never have escaped Erasmus, who was so conversant with its manners and inhabitants. But the illus-
trious

trious Essayist is far from being of the same opinion with him: he censures the custom as disgusting and disagreeable, and derives from it many ill consequences: which is no matter of wonder, when I am informed that he had lived above half a century at the time he gave his opinion, and consequently had reached that period of life, which is too cold and inanimate to be affected by possession, much more by a single touch of a hand or a lip. He speaks, therefore, as satiated, and as all old people do, who have lost their relish and enjoyment of those pleasures which are derived from passion: whereas Erasmus was but in his thirtieth year, in the full meridian of manhood; in a country too where the women rival the rest of the universe in beauty: how could he then but commend a custom so favorable to ideas which inspire the mind with delight, enthusiasm, and love? I do not know any greater proof of the superior beauty of our countrywomen, than that they could fire the cold and lifeless soul of a Dutchman to exclaim, " Suaviorum plena sunt omnia;" and yet I think he deserved every thing their beauty could grant, who could describe what he felt

from

from its effect, in such delightful and elegant language, and was so sensible of their excelling charms. When I consider the *divinis, blandæ, exciperis, demitteris, redduntur & propinantur suavia, dividuntur, affatim*, and that delicious *moveas*, parent of the inchanting *Suaviorum plena sunt omnia*; I cannot but admire the continued vigour of the sentence; where there is nothing forced, nothing languishing and feeble, but the genuine voice of nature and eloquence. " Contextus totus virilis est, non sunt circa " flosculos occupati." The sense illuminates and produces the words; not words of air, but of strength and manliness, signifying more than they express. I am not sufficiently acquainted with the history of Erasmus, to tell in what part of Great-Britain the ladies drew from him such high encomiums; but I should imagine he applied it to the Scotch ladies, as he spent a considerable time in Scotland, was rhetoric tutor to one of the king's sons, and afterwards archbishop of St. Andrew's: besides, the custom was always more prevalent here than in England. But the reason which weighs most is, that he mentions the Scotch women in other parts of his work, in the most favourable terms;

terms; and proves, from his warm and animated expreffions, that he was not infenfible, though a philofopher and an archbifhop, to that beauty which is peculiar to this country, and which is fo extreme, that a falute is almoft invaluable. After having quoted fo learned an authority in favour of this cuftom, you may think it prefumption in me to offer any thing againft it; but I cannot help saying, however delightful it may be to the male part of our fpecies, however productive of tender and agreeable fenfations, they ought to confider that it very feldom happens that the falute is a voluntary one, and it frequently is the caufe of difguft and embarraffment to the fair fex. But the ftrongeft circumftances againft it is, that by the conftant practice of it, it takes away that amiable modefty, that " metuitque tangi nuptiarum expers," which is one of the moft enchanting allurements, and gives them an appearance of forwardnefs and boldnefs in their addrefs, which borders on indelicacy. When I fee a beautiful girl of fixteen approaching to be faluted by a row of ftrangers, it always gives me an idea of tafting before you bid; and removes from my imagination that *semi-reducta* appearance, which Ovid, the great master of the Art of Love, mentions as so pleasing in the figure of Venus, and so essential to real beauty. I think nothing need be said more in dispraise of any custom, than that it diminishes the appearance of modesty in the fair sex; which, in the language of a celebrated author, " gives " a maid greater beauty than even the bloom " of youth, bestows on the wife the dignity of " a matron, and re-instates the widow in her " virginity." But there is one other charm of which it deprives them, and by so doing, is very detrimental to society, by stealing from lovers and husbands a pleasure, in which there is no little delight and enjoyment: the young ladies become so habituated to salutes, and by experience so practised in their manœuvres, that their sensations are perfectly hebetated and dull; and, instead of finding those emotions and satisfaction which the breath of an inamorato inspires in other countries, the warmest embraces, and most fervent kiss can make no impression on their affection, nor is able to rouse the latent spark of sensibility and desire. By this means, love loses half its artillery.

The

The passions of the men are inflamed: they rush forward to unnatural modes of seduction, and, by every desperate contrivance, endeavour " to rob the tender virgins of their hearts."

Consider also, you who are blessed with every conjugal endearment, how languid and insipid must be the marriage bed, when incapable of deriving pleasures from this source? For surely there is no finer sensation than the electric fire which is communicated by the lips of the object of our affection; except that of knowing that it is reciprocal: and yet much fewer evils are brought on mankind by this effect of salutations, than if they operated in a contrary manner; for then, I believe, that the married gentlemen in particular would have greater cause to lament, were we by any means to endeavour to increase the natural sensibility of the ladies: so that we must still agree with Doctor Pangloss's system; and, though we may experience many disagreeable things in this variegated world, confess, after all, " that " every thing is for the best."

I remain your ever affectionate friend, and obliged, humble servant.

LETTER VI.

Character of the Scotch in some Points mistaken. Some Observations upon them.

To R. D. Esq;

Edinburgh, December 2, 1774.

SIR,

THE civilities that have been paid to my fellow-traveller and me, the politeness we have met with, and the attentions with which we have been honoured since our arrival, all conspire to make this country every day more agreeable. At first I was afraid we should become too popular; but that fear has now subsided, and we walk along without notice.

The common people of this place, who had only seen travellers pass through, like birds of passage in their way to the Highlands or the Hebrides, were astonished to find two people become stationary at Edinburgh for a whole winter. "What were we come for?" was the first question. "They presumed, to "study physic?" "No." "To study law?" "No,"

" No." " Then it muſt be divinity?" " No."
" Very odd," they ſaid, " that we ſhould come
" to Edinburgh without one of theſe reaſons."
At one time we were ſuppoſed to be hair-dreſ-
ſers, at another, mountebanks, at a third, players. Whilſt this ſuppoſition laſted, we were in
great repute. A thouſand people, who would
have let us paſs unnoticed as peaceable and
quiet gentlemen, the moment they imagined we
might ſome day exhibit before them, naturally concluded we muſt have ſomething very
curious about us, and that they had a right to
look at us. In ſhort, we have undergone as
many changes as Proteus, in the imaginations
of other people. One very pious lady, who had
long been torturing her invention to no purpoſe, concluded we could have come for no
good, and very charitably wiſhed we were
well out of the place. In ſpite of all theſe
conjectures, however, here we are, and here
we are likely to remain for ſome time. Our
pride, at leaſt, will not let us remove till we
have convinced them, " that we are no ſpies,
" but true men." If they did themſelves juſtice, they would have no reaſon to be ſur-
prized. Is it ſo ſtrange and unnatural, that

Engliſhmen

Englishmen should visit Scotland? or that, when they are there, they should have no inclination to leave it?

I have not as yet been long enough in this country to have formed many observations on the manners of the people; but the general opinion which the English entertain, that they are laborious and œconomical, seems to be very erroneous. The common people, who, as long as the Clans subsisted, were entirely governed by martial laws, and from their infancy attached to arms, and who knew no other ambition but that of signalizing themselves in contests for their lairds, could feel no predilection for one spot of ground, nor possess any settled habitation. No one would be inclined to throw away his labour in cultivating a barren and thankless soil, when he was liable to be robbed of the fruits of his industry every moment. This insecurity of property soon introduced an hereditary aversion to labour; and they preferred trusting to what force or stratagem might bring them, rather than to a patient course of industry, which was so subject to be interrupted. In no country whatever, where the love of arms is predominant,

nant, the people are known to be fond of agriculture. A Roman conful might poffibly go from the plough to command an army; but fuppofing it to be true, it is only an exception, not a rule. The fpirit which actuates a foldier is no more adapted to make a good farmer, than the fpot, which is the fubject of contention, can be favourable to the labours of the hufbandman. *Auferre, trucidare, rapere, falfis nominibus, belli gloriâ, atque ubi folitudinem facit, pacem appellat.* Such is the character which Tacitus gives of this military fpirit, and he had many opportunities of obferving its effects.

Though the diffolution of the Clans, and fome little improvements that have been made, have in fome meafure broke this general contempt for labour, which the Highlanders once entertained, they are ftill what a Dutchman, or even an Englifhman would call very idle. An Highlander will, to this day, wrap himfelf up in his plaid, throw himfelf at his length on the ground, and lie there totally unconcerned, while his wife and children are bufily employed in getting in the fcanty harveft which the barren nature of his land allows

allows him. He will neither fully his dignity nor his lands in such dirty work. It is in vain to oppose these national prejudices with argument; for reason and even interest sink before them. . Every people have some of them, and many of them boast of these absurdities as honourable distinctions. The Spanish writers tell you, with great marks of applause, that their monarch Philip IV. never made the least motion with his eyes in giving audience, nor was ever seen to laugh in his whole life. Is it not almost incredible that human folly could ever have been carried to such a length?

Tho' the tradesmen and artists of this country now begin to find the benefits of industry, they are far from being frugal: in general they live up to the amount of their incomes; and you see as many bankruptcies in proportion in an Edinburgh Newspaper, as you do in a London Gazette. Here likewise, as in London, they know the art of extracting advantage from ruin; and frequently find, as a witty writer observes, ' that a commission of bank-
' ruptcy is the best commission they could
' have.' This early introduction of luxury and
dissipation

dissipation is somewhat extraordinary. When people have acquired some degree of fortune, by a toilsome and unbroken course of industry, they understand in general the value of money too well ever to be tempted to throw it away again. As yet they have had no immense riches accumulated by trade, nor any nabobs to introduce eastern modes of luxury; so that this premature taste for dissipation is not so easy to be accounted for. The people of landed property have, in general, outrun their estates; but the reason here is obvious: tho' the Clanship is abolished, the dependents still remain, and every man who had neither inclination nor ability to do any thing, thought he had a right to be supported by his superior. This was carried so far, that many of them have been obliged to leave the country, and fix their residence at Edinburgh. Accustomed, however, to an ostentatious display of riches, and to a parade which was easily supported in the country, they have given too much into the same fashion, in a place where the expence attending it must be ruinous; and many of the first people have found it so. The young men of fashion here follow the examples of their

neighbours

neighbours in England; tho', I believe, the present fashionable mode with us, of raising money upon their own lives, has not as yet travelled so far. There is no trafficking with Jews here; for, what is marvellous to tell, there never was a Jew seen in this country; they and their annuities are yet in reversion.

But what will surprize a stranger the most on entering this country, will be the immense number of people he will find of the same name. An English gentleman who had travelled over the greatest part of Argyleshire in quest of a Mr. Campbel (which is here pronounced Camel) said, it was in vain to hunt after him any longer, for there were as many Camels here as on the desarts of Arabia. It is frequently no sign of your having found out the person you want, when you are acquainted both with his name and title: you must likewise know from whence he comes, or you know nothing. Now and then indeed a celebrated Beauty occurs, who may be found out without her designation. Should you speak of Miss J———n, for instance, every one will know who you mean, without saying she comes from H———n.

The Laird of a place is generally diftinguifhed by the name of his Eftate, and frequently by no other appellation. This derivation of names from the place of their abode is fimilar to that cuftom amongft the Germans, who are always named after their caftles, their demefnes, manors, eftates, &c. &c. and who, like Cadwallader, have a name as long as your arm, and a pedigree older than the flood.

This country has long been celebrated for its hofpitality to ftrangers: and I am fure I can, with great truth, add my humble fuffrage to this general obfervation. They do not think they have paid you all the attention that is neceffary, when they have invited you once to dinner, and then take no more notice of you: they are eager to fhew you repeated civilities; they are happy to explain, to inform you of what is really curious in their country; they give you a general invitation to their houfes; they beg of you to vifit them familiarly, and are forry if you do not do fo. I am afhamed to fay that many of my countrymen feem to have forgot all their kindnefs the moment they returned over the Tweed. I

truft

truſt thoſe waters will never waſh away my remembrance, but that I ſhall always be proud to own the hoſpitality of the Scotch, and the civilities I received in Scotland.

I have the honour to be, &c.

LETTER VII.

On the Good-breeding of the Scotch; their Language, particular Beauties in it, and Expreſſions.

To the Honourable William S——, Eſq.

Edinburgh, December 6, 1774.

DEAR SIR,

I Know of no quality more conſpicuous in the inhabitants of this country, than Complaiſance; which is common to every age and ſex, but more particularly to the women, who ſeem to make it a ſtudy to oblige, and endeavour to emulate each other in good-breeding: which, I think, is the art of ſhewing people, by external ſigns, the inward regard which we have for them. As nothing
indicates

indicates the judgment of a nation more than good-breeding; so it likewise difcovers their good nature: for politenefs is, in my opinion, the refult not only of good nature, but good fenfe; it gives a luftre to every other charm, and conceals, in a great degree, every difadvantage which women may lie under in their perfons. But I affure you, the Scotch ladies have no need of this enchanting accomplifhment, on the laft account. Nature has been as liberal to them in decorating their external parts, as in ornamenting their minds; and I believe as few nations excel them in beauty, as in advantages derived from difpofition and education. No women underftand better the rules of decorum, nor are they rivalled by the French in the talent of agreeable converfation; for which they feem to be better calculated, as well from their fuperior knowledge of the world, as from their more extenfive acquaintance with books and literature.

It is common with the Scotch to make ufe of the word *Friend*, even to ftrangers, after the manner of the French nation; which I have often

often thought conveyed an idea of benevolence and philanthropy most conciliating; and which prejudiced you in their favour at first interview. They frequently also address you in conversation with the appellation of *my dear Sir*, the *mio caro Signiore* of the Italians: which, you must needs acknowledge, is a never-failing argument, and, at first onset, immediately disarms an antagonist, notwithstanding the rage and passion of disputation. It carries with it this peculiar advantage, that disputes, by this means, never arrive at such a pitch, as to occasion a downright quarrel, which is too often the case in many countries, and, I am sorry to say, too general in ours; where, from a conceited education, and narrow intercourse with mankind, an impatience of contradiction, and a readiness to contradict, is too apt to usher in a disputation with downright abuse, or the appearance of open enmity. But when a man stops you short with *my good friend*, or *my dear sir*, you cannot but be as calm as when you first began; because the words themselves imply a truce, and consequently whatever follows must be looked on

as

as well intended, and with no hostile meaning; and delivered as the real sentiments of the speaker, without that glee for disputation, which is so absurd and unpolite. There is also another great advantage derived from it: It not only prevents the violence of argument, but, by so doing, renders the faculties clear and undisturbed, makes a man master of the reasoning he has already collected, and gives him time and opportunity to invent others, which may arise from the arguments or language of his opponent: and, in short, if you are vanquished, you cannot but admire the lenity of your enemy; and, on the contrary, cannot triumph over those, who submit with so much good grace and manners. If, then, you confess it is persuasive in the men, it is certainly invincible in the fair sex, who, with *my dear sir* added to their other artillery, are sure to obtain every thing they can wish. When you are told that, on the first introduction to a lady in this country, you are favoured with a salute, which immediately discovers the fragrance of her breath, the downy velvet of her skin, and pearly enamel of her teeth; that the first word which she utters to you is either *my good friend*, or *my dear sir*, which, softened by the sweetness of her voice, and affability of her manner, must receive an additional degree of warmth, and kindness; can you wonder that I am so enamoured with their company? or rather, do you not wonder that I can think of leaving them? But alas! alas! the time approaches for my departure: and if it was not for one dear object, who attracts me, like the faithful steel, to the magic circle of her arms, it would be with the utmost regret I should bid farewell to a country, which is the land of Pleasure, Rapture, and Delight. But suppose you should say, that these words, though very pleasing at first on account of their novelty, must soon lose their charm, when we come to be acquainted, that they are mere words of custom and ceremony, and uttered without any intention of good-will or sincerity; and that expressions of kindness, when they are not known to be the marks and effects of kindness, are empty sounds; I must grant, that by degrees they become habitual, and do not operate so strongly by use, as on a stranger.

ger. But surely, at any time they are the highest signs of complaisance; and giving the appearance of truth to actions, and a strong desire to please and oblige, certainly produce a partiality for the speaker: not by the words, which in common speech signify scarce any thing; but because by these words he shews that he thinks you worth notice. Expressions of this nature are ingenious flattery: it makes those to whom it is paid, flatter themselves, whilst they look on it as a declaration of merit in themselves: and pray, what mortal man does not love to be flattered by a lady? For my own part, if it is a fault, I must plead guilty; and though I detest it as much as hypocrisy in the male part of our species, I am not proof against it when assisted by the fire of sparkling eyes, and delivered by female eloquence. A staunch philosopher would derive this credulity from the original perverseness of human nature; and in the same manner as Adam swallowed the forbidden fruit, though he knew it contained none of those excellent qualities ascribed to it by Eve; so we, his progeny, are tempted by the flattery of the fair sex, and are sure to give it credit, notwithstanding we are conscious of its untruth and insincerity.

The Scotch language has one beauty, in which it greatly excels the English, and in which also it conforms to the Italian; that of diminutives, which are created at pleasure, and expressed in one word, by the addition of a letter or syllable: thus, they say "manny, "doggy, catty," for a little man, dog, or cat; "wifey," for a little wife; and if it was necessary to speak of an inanimate thing, they do it also in the same manner; as "a "buckley, knifey, booky, housey," for a little buckle, knife, book, and house. I need not tell you how emphatical this makes their tongue, and what an improvement it is on ours. But their pronunciation and accent is far from being agreeable: it gives an air of gravity, sedateness, and importance to their words; which, though of use sometimes in an harangue or public discourse, in common conversation seems dull, heavy, stupid, and unharmonious. On which account I scarcely ever heard a Scotchman tell a good story in all

my

my life; for, notwithstanding he might put in all the circumstances to work it to a point, he would be sure to spoil it by his deficiency in manner, and remove the sting, which ought to tickle the imagination of the hearer, by appearing not to feel it himself. The inhabitants of this place, who are acquainted with the English, are sensible of this, and endeavour to speak like them, especially the politer sort of people, and the Professors of the College, who, in their lectures, strive to shake off the Scotch pronunciation as much as possible. Your perfect acquaintance with the literary productions of this country, makes it unnecessary for me to make any observations on their style. I shall only say, that they appear to me, from their conversation, to write English as a foreign tongue; their mode of talking, phrase, and expression, but little resembling the language of their works; though I cannot but add, that even some of them, in their conversation, are fond of shewing their learning, by making use of words derived from ancient languages. Amœnity is a favourite word of a celebrated Historian, who is

truly

truly the boaſt of his country; who, in private reputation, has as few equals, as in public, ſuperiors; and whoſe works may be juſtly ſaid to be *non ludrica cantilena ad momentum temporis, ſed monumentum ad æternitatem.*

Believe me your ever affectionate friend,

and obliged, humble ſervant.

LETTER VIII.

On the Executions in Scotland.

To R. D. Eſq.

Edinburgh, December 9, 1774.

SIR,

I Was this morning a witneſs to one of the moſt ſolemn and mournful of all ſpectacles, the execution of a criminal. The ſight of death is always affecting; but it becomes ſtill more moving, when we behold a poor wretch ſacrificed to the injured laws of his country, without

without one eye to compaſſionate his diſtreſs, or one friend who will own him, and expiring amidſt a rude multitude, who probably inſult him in his laſt moments.

When I was at Paris, it was my misfortune to be an involuntary witneſs of the ſufferings of a poor wretch, who was broke upon the wheel for the murder of his brother. It is almoſt impoſſible, in my opinion, to conceive a death more ſhocking; but the little concern the people ſeemed to feel upon the occaſion, and their avidity to behold ſo terrible a ſight, were ſtill more aſtoniſhing. A poor woman, who had a very good place for ſeeing, at laſt fainted under the agitations which the ſufferings of the poor criminal occaſioned; and the people behind, inſtead of aſſiſting her, were entirely taken up with the thoughts of getting her place, and ſeeing at their eaſe.

In the diſpoſition which a criminal is ſuppoſed to be in at ſuch a moment, when the fears of death are immediate, the inſtruments already before his eyes, and the many and terrible objects to engage his attention; at ſuch a ſeaſon, I cannot but think the ceremonies of religion ill-timed. When the poor creature
was

was already tied down upon the cross, a *Religieux* was very busy in making him repeat little prayers for the repose of his soul; and when he had undergone the dreadful ceremony of having every limb broken, and was taken from the cross to be tied on the wheel, when every joint was streaming with blood, and himself expiring in the last agonies of pain, the attention of the clergyman was engaged, not with the sufferings of the poor criminal, but in making him kiss a little piece of wood in the shape of a cross. During this ceremony, I did not observe one tear shed: they remarked, indeed, that the criminal was very wellm ade, and that " *Monsieur le Bourreau étoit bien adroit.*"

In Scotland, and I mention it to its honour, there is, on these unhappy occasions, much more solemnity and decency observed. The lenity of the laws here makes it necessary that a man shall be " habit and repute" a thief, before he can be condemned to die for theft; and therefore executions, except for murder, are very uncommon. This man had already been twice convicted and pardoned; so that there was no room for intercession to the King's

King's mercy; nor was there the leaſt hope of his amendment, as he was near ſixty years old, had ſpent the whole of his life in a ſeries of repeated thefts, and as he advanced in age, had advanced likewiſe in iniquity.

The town of Edinburgh, from the amazing height of its buildings, ſeems peculiarly formed to make a ſpectacle of this kind ſolemn and affecting. The houſes, from the bottom up to the top, were lined with people, every window crowded with ſpectators to ſee the unfortunate man paſs by. At one o'clock the City Guard went to the door of the Tolbooth, the common gaol here, to receive and conduct their priſoner to the place of execution, which is always in the Graſs Market, at a very great diſtance from the priſon. All the remaining length of the High Street was filled with people, not only from the town itſelf, but the country around, whom the novelty of the ſight had brought together. On the Guard knocking at the door of the Tolbooth, the unhappy criminal made his appearance. He was dreſſed in a white waiſtcoat and breeches, uſual on theſe occaſions, bound with black ribands, and a night-cap tied with the ſame.

His

His white hairs, which were spread over his face, made his appearance still more pitiable. Two clergymen walked on each side of him, and were discoursing with him on subjects of religion. The executioner, who seemed ashamed of the meanness of his office, followed muffled up in a great coat, and the City Guards, with their arms ready, marched around him. The criminal, whose hands were tied behind him, and the rope about his neck, walked up the remaining part of the street. It is the custom in this country for the criminal to walk to the gallows, which has something much more decent in it than being thrown into a cart, as in England, and carried, like a beast, to slaughter. The slow, pensive, melancholy step of a man in these circumstances, has something in it that seems to accord with affliction, and affects the mind forcibly with its distress. It is the pace which a man in sorrow naturally falls into: " Omnis enim motus animi," says Cicero, " suum quendam à naturâ habet vultum, et " sonum, et gestum; totumque corpus homi- " nis, et ejus omnis vultus, omnesque voces, ut " nervi in fidibus, ita sonant, ut à motu animi " sint pulsæ."

When

When the criminal had descended three parts of the hill which leads to the Grass Market, he beheld the crowd waiting for his coming, and the instrument of execution at the end of it. He made a short stop here, naturally shocked at such a sight, and the people seemed to sympathize with his affliction. When he reached the end, he recalled his resolution; and, after passing some time in prayer with the clergyman, and once addressing himself to the people, he was turned off, and expired.

I own I cannot bear that unmoved temper in death, which has distinguished some people. The fear of dying is, in my opinion, a principle of our nature, implanted in us for the preservation of our existence, and which ought to be relinquished only with life. If ever we overcome this principle, it is when the mind is absorbed in grief, or insensible to its own condition. The Duke de la Rochefoucault says, " That they who are executed affect " sometimes a constancy and contempt of " death, which is in fact nothing more than " a fear to look upon it; so that this con- " stancy may be said to be to the mind what
" a ban-

"a bandage is to the eyes." The voice of reasoning, if such is its voice, can never be regarded in these last and painful moments; nor have I any opinion of that miserable philosophy, which would render us indifferent, when we behold the affliction of our friends, when we are separated from every thing we esteem in life, and when we are about to experience that " something after death," of whose nature we are all uncertain.

So great is the abhorrence of the office of executioner in this country, that the poor wretch is obliged to be kept three or four days in prison, till the hatred of the mob has subsided, and his act is forgotten. Mr. Boswell, who congratulates Corsica on this proof of innocence, may pay his own countrymen the same compliment. If, however, there was any reasoning against popular prejudices, they must acknowledge, that an office, which is so necessary, must be imposed on some one; and therefore, to insult the poor animal, whose calamities oblige him to a duty so requisite for the safety of society, is highly unbecoming that spirit of humanity, and that gentleness

ness of manners which every polished people ought to cultivate.

If they consider this as a point of honour, it is a false one. Soldiers, who are more governed by that principle than any other set of men, act very differently: they hold it no dishonour, when they are commanded to inflict in person the punishment of death on a fellow-soldier for cowardice, mutiny, or desertion; nor do they think it any disgrace to others, who are ordered to the same duty.

I beg pardon for detaining you so long on so melancholy a subject, when the present rage of being lively excludes all objects of grief, and, I much fear, even of feeling. I own there is a pleasure, to my apprehension, even in sorrow, and in making the distresses of others our own. I hate to be reduced to the necessity of wondering why I have wept; and I never feel more real indignation, than after the representation of an affecting tragedy, when the heart becomes interested with its descriptions, and every finer feeling is excited, in comes a man dancing with a straw upon his nose, or balancing a glass bottle.

I have the honour to be, &c.

LETTER

LETTER IX.

The Suppers of the Scotch, and their Manner of conducting them.

To R. D. Esq;

Edinburgh, December 12, 1774.

SIR,

A Man who visits this country, after having been in France, will find, in a thousand instances, the resemblance which there is betwixt these two nations. That air of mirth and vivacity, that quick and penetrating look, that spirit of gaiety which distinguishes the French, is equally visible in the Scotch. It is the character of the nation; and it is a very happy one, as it makes them disregard even their poverty. Where there is any material difference, I believe it may be attributed to the difference of their religion; for that same Catholic religion, to say the truth of it, is a most comfortable one. The article of absolution is certainly a blessed invention, and renders the spirits free and unclouded, by placing

all

all the burthen of our sins upon another man's back. A poor Englishman goes fretting and groaning, and carrying his miserable face into all companies, as contagious as an epidemical disorder, without one soul to take compassion on him, or pity his weakness: and should he not have a wife or family at home who cannot avoid him, he finds no person who will bear his infirmities, or look as sad as he does; but is constrained to wander about an unsociable being, till the month of November, and the *maladie Angloise*, relieve him from his distresses.

But though the Scotch have no absolution, they have something very like it—a superstitious reliance on the efficacy of going constantly to church. Many of them may be said to pass half their lives there; for they go almost without ceasing, and look as sorrowful at the time as if they were going, not only to bury their sins, but themselves. At other hours, they are as chearful and as gay as possible: and, probably, from hence arises that ease, that spirit in their conversation, which charms in every company, and which is the life of every society. They

F see

see no harm in innocent familiarity. They think a frank and unrestrained behaviour the best sign of a good heart; and agree with Lord Shaftesbury, " that gravity is the " very essence of imposture."

Whenever the Scotch of both sexes meet, they do not appear as if they had never seen each other before, or wished never to see each other again: they do not sit in sullen silence, looking on the ground, biting their nails, and at a loss what to do with themselves; and, if some one should be hardy enough to break silence, start, as if they were shot through the ear with a pistol: but they address each other at first sight, and with an *impressement* that is highly pleasing; they appear to be satisfied with one another, or at least, if they really are not so, they have the prudence to conceal their dislike. To see them in perfection, is to see them at their entertainments.

When dinners are given here, they are invitations of form. The entertainment of pleasure is their suppers, which resemble the *petit soupers* of France. Of these they are very fond; and it is a mark of their friendship

ship to be admitted to be of the party. It is in these meetings that the pleasures of society and conversation reign, when the restraints of ceremony are banished, and you see people really as they are: and I must say, in honour of the Scotch, that I never met with a more agreeable people, with more pleasing or more insinuating manners, in my life. These little parties generally consist of about seven or eight persons, which prevents the conversation from being particular, and which it always must be in larger companies. During the supper, which continues some time, the Scotch Ladies drink more wine than an English woman could well bear; but the climate requires it, and probably in some measure it may enliven their natural vivacity. Without quoting foreign authorities, you will allow that a certain degree of wine adds great life to conversation. An Englishman, we know, is sometimes esteemed the best companion in the world after the second bottle; and who, before that, would not have opened his lips for the universe. After supper is removed, and they are tired of conversing, they vary the scene by singing, in which many of the Scotch excel. There is a plaintive simplicity in the generality of their songs, to which the words are extremely well adapted, and which, from the mouth of a pretty Scotch girl, is inconceivably attracting. You frequently feel the force of those very expressions, that at another time you would not understand, when they are sung by a young person whose inclinations and affections are frequently expressed in the terms made use of, and which the heart claims as its own. The eye, the whole countenance speak frequently as much as the voice; for I have sometimes found, that I had a very just idea of the tenor of a song, though I did not comprehend three words in the whole.

Formerly it was the custom for the bagpipe to play during their entertainments, and every family had their bard. In these songs were rehearsed the martial and heroic deeds of their ancestors, as incentives to their own courage; but in these piping times of peace, " our stern alarms have changed to " merry meetings," and tales of love and gentleness have succeeded to those of war. Instead of

the

the drowſy hum of a bagpipe, which would certainly have laid my noble courage aſleep, the voice of ſome pretty girl claims your attention, which, in my opinion, is no bad change. I muſt confeſs, I have not much opinion of thoſe feaſts " of other times," where your ears were continually ſtunned with the murders ſuch a man had committed, and where he was to be continually told of what he had already done, that he might perform the ſame again. His modeſty muſt certainly be put out of the queſtion, otherwiſe he never could have ſat to hear a detail of his own deeds. It is obſerved of a Welch hero, " that he was a devout man, " a great warrior, and an excellent piper; " and that he could play, with great ſkill, " the ſongs of all his actions." This is ſtill better—With ſuch authority, ought any man to be blamed for talking of himſelf, and being the hero of his own tale? While every one is railing at the preſent times, it is ſome conſolation to find, that in many inſtances our forefathers were as abſurd as we are; and that if we poſſeſs little, we have at leaſt the negative merit of not boaſting of what we have,

have. I own I feel a pleasure in reconciling us to ourselves; for, as some ingenious writers have proved that we are every way inferior to our ancestors, since we cannot rise to them, the only way left is to bring them down to us.

I have the honour to be, &c.

LETTER X.

On the Civility of the Common People.

To the Reverend Dr. ———

DEAR SIR,   Edinburgh, December 15, 1774.

YOU will wonder to see a letter from me from this place, my last having been from London, without any thoughts of such a journey. You should have heard from me before this time, if I could as easily have found the knowledge of your residence, as the disposition of cultivating your

your correspondence; which I have always carried about me, since I have had the happiness of being acquainted with you personally.

You are pleased to say, my observations on the uncultivated manners and innate roughness of the common people, in many of the counties in England, entirely agreed with yours, when you made the tour of our country. It gave me much pleasure to hear you said so; and I shall hereafter have a higher opinion of my own judgment, from its coinciding with yours. I find the vulgar inhabitants of this country as varying in their dispositions from those of the southern parts of Great Britain, as the Æthiopians from the natives of Mexico, and as unlike, as if they were Antipodes. Though Scotland and England together are very minute in comparison with any of the countries on the European Continent, yet you cannot conceive a greater dissimilarity of manners; and so wide is the difference, that you would think the distance between them was from heaven to earth. I speak of the common people only;

only; for the polished and polite are nearly the same in many respects.

Instead of that stubborn rudeness, and uncouth mind, that shyness and barbarism, which is even cultivated by our peasants, and which before I so much complained of, you find in the lowest hind in Scotland a compliant obsequiousness, and softness of temper, an ambition to oblige, and a sociability which charms you. They are naturally grave, hospitable, and friendly; and have such a peculiar attachment to their own country and families, that, were I to relate to you the wonderful accounts which I have listened to with astonishment, you could not but think that I was bordering on romance. But what distinguishes them from the vulgar inhabitants of almost any nation, is that peculiar desire to oblige and instruct; a philanthropy which they discover, on all occasions, to be of service and to do good, and which never can fail of rendering their intercourse and conversation most agreeable, and of the greatest utility to the traveller. In a wild and uncultivated country, in a miserable hovel,

destitute

destitute of every convenience of life, exposed to all the inclemencies of climate, without common necessaries to drag on a wretched, uncomfortable being, it is here you meet with souls generous, contented, and happy, ever ready to the call of humanity; religious, and charitable. In a short tour that I lately made to the Highlands, an opportunity presented itself of making my observations on the minds of this people; since I mixed with them, conversed on variety of subjects, lived in their families, and passed with them many a happy hour. As I frequently wandered over the mountains with my gun, I often found a sequestered village, which had little communication with the rest of mankind, that had received scarce any form or fashion from art and human invention; and consequently, not far remote from its original simplicity. One day a storm drove me to seek shelter in a small cottage, which I by chance espied in a deep valley at the foot of one of their mountains; and on entering, I saw a venerable old woman, with another about thirty, and five or six pretty infants, which, by their resemblance, I easily discovered to

be

be her children; all employed in some domestic concern, and waiting the return of the master of the family, who, I afterwards found, was gone to provide fish and other necessaries, from a small town on the banks of the neighbouring lake. When they perceived me at the door, the mother of the little ones came immediately to meet me, and, with a countenance full of benevolence and hospitality, saluted me in the Earse language; which, though I did not understand it, seemed to welcome me to whatever they could afford, or I could expect to find there. She then reached me a stool, which was made of rushes, seeing I did not comprehend her tongue, and was pointing to me to sit down by the fire, when I addressed myself to the old lady in the corner, and demanded whether she could speak English; but they all shook their heads, and were silent. I then unloaded my game-bag, which contained a white hare, and some ptarmigan, and began to court their good opinion, by presenting them to the children, and endeavouring to divert them, by shewing them my shooting implements, and other things which I had

in

in my pocket, and which seemed to give them much delight; the woman, in the mean time, making signs to me to pull off my wet cloaths, and holding out a plaid which they had warmed by the fire. On my seeming to refuse their kind offices, they shook themselves, and looked sorrowful; which meant, as I since learnt, if I did not change my dress, I should catch an ague; a disorder to which they were extremely subject.

As the weather continued to threaten, and night was not far off, I sat myself down by the hearth, and amused myself by pulling off the feathers of one of the birds, which I made them comprehend would be very acceptable, as I had eat nothing almost the whole day; and just as I was preparing to broil it, the highlander opened the door, and, expressing his surprise at finding a stranger had taken possession of his household goods, in a free and good-natured tone of voice, in the Scotch language, begged of me to proceed in my employ; and enquired the reason of this visit; adding, with a smile, ‘ that I must have en-
‘ tertained his wife and mother extremely well
‘ during his absence, to become so familiar
‘ with

' with them; especially as they did not un-
' derstand me, and had never in their lives
' beheld the face of any human person, ex-
' cept a few of their own Clan, who inha-
' bited the other side of the hill.' When I
had told him my story, and entreated pardon
for the freedom I had taken, he embraced me
with the highest degree of rapture, and, or-
dering the others to do the same, told me,
' the gentleman with whom I had been, and to
' whose house I wished to return the next day,
' was the head of his Clan; that he respected
' him, and would die for him; and, since I
' was a visiter to the Laird, I claimed from
' him every kind of hospitality and conve-
' nience, which his poor pittance could
' supply: though,' he added, ' as a stranger
' who had lost my way, I had a right to
' civility and assistance from every man.'
When I had finished my ptarmigan, of which
they would none of them partake, he produced on the table some dried fish, cheese,
and oat-cake, of which they all eat with an
appetite that discovered their poverty, and
that brought to my remembrance the saying
of the philosopher, that " He that eats with

" an

" an empty stomach, needs no variety of
" food; he that drinks only for thirst, desires
" least change of liquor; and he that wants
" least, comes nearest to the Gods." On our
being satisfied, he gave some to the infants,
and said a grace in the presbyterian form,
praising God with more fervent devotion than
ever I met with in an English bishop at the
administration of the sacrament.

The rest of the night we spent in conversation, whilst they plied me heartily with whisky; and I answered a number of questions which were demanded of me by the women, through him as interpreter; till at length, overpowered by fatigue, I reposed myself in a plaid by the fire; and enjoyed as sound a slumber as if my head had been pillowed on down,

" Under a canopy of costly state."

The morning arose, and I took farewel of my kind hostesses; who parted with me with many expressions of friendship; and, if I may judge from their countenance, wished that the stormy weather had continued, that I might have been detained longer. The highlander accompanied

accompanied me acrofs the mountains in my progrefs homeward, cheating the drearinefs of the way by his entertaining difcourfe, concerning the antiquity of his family, and the anceftors of his Laird; whom he had followed in the rebellion, and under whofe banners he had ventured his life and fortune. We had now arrived within fight of the houfe of my friend, when he wifhed me health, and fuccefs through life, and that I might never go further out of my right way, than when I wandered to his habitation. I paid his kindnefs with all the coin I was then mafter of, and parted with a thoufand thanks and gratitude for his civilities.

I have detained you all this while with this length of ftory, in order to paint to you the true character of a Scotch peafant; and I dare fay you will be aftonifhed to find fo many virtues in a family in the Highlands, where the inhabitants are thought by us to be in a ftate of barbarifm. But fuch, I affure you, they all are,

" Extrema per illos,
" Juftitia excedens terris vefligia fecit."

Even in Edinburgh, the fame fpirit runs through

through the common people; who are infinitely more civil, humanized, and hospitable, than any I ever met with. Every one is ready to serve and assist a stranger; they shew the greatest respect to a person superior to them; and you never receive an impertinent answer. But, after all this, I wish I could say they were more happy: notwithstanding these many excellencies, I find lying, treachery, dissimulation, envy, detraction, and vice, have their respective significations. As to their country, it is beautiful, and grand to a miracle, and, though far from being temperate, is so healthy, that you hear of fewer disorders than amongst any other people; and I declare, in every part that I have been, I never saw either an exceedingly deformed person, or an aged, toothless, paralytic highlander. They eat a great quantity of fish dried in the sun, and a cake made of oatmeal, baked hard and flat. Their constant liquor is whisky; which is also made from oats, has a quick taste, extremely heady, but comfortable to the stomach; unpalatable to strangers, though hot and nourishing to those that are used to it.

And

And now, my good friend, I must take my leave of you, wishing you may enjoy your new preferment many a day. I think you want nothing now to add to your dignity, but an infant boy, and to be called father; which, take my word for it, is infinitely more grateful than a pair of lawn sleeves, or the popedom in the character of an old bachelor.

My best respects attend Mrs. ——; and believe me

Your ever sincere friend,
and obliged, humble servant.

LETTER XI.

On the Genius of the Natives; their Temper; Perfons; Hofpitality; Inquifitivenefs about Strangers. — The Impoffibility of being conccaled. — Affifted by the Society of Cadies.

To the Honourable Lord ———

Edinburgh, December 25, 1774.

DEAR SIR,

I Have continued in this City ever fince you laft heard from me, and find it fo agreeable, that I forefee it will be with difficulty I fhall prevail on myfelf to leave it. The inhabitants have fo much civility and hofpitality, and the favours which I receive are fo many, that it would argue a want of acknowledgment, and that I am unworthy of the good opinion they are fo kind to entertain, did I wifh to haften my departure. Your arguments, I muft confefs, carry great weight with them; and I muft trouble you to deliver my obligations to my friends, for lamenting my long abfence. I am fure they would readily

dily pardon my neglect, were they as sensible of the charms of Scotland: for I find here every thing I can wish; and must own, I never spent my time more to my satisfaction. The gentlemen of this nation (pardon my impartiality) are infinitely better calculated for an agreeable society than Englishmen; as they have the spirit of the French without their grimace, with much more learning, and more modesty, mixed with that philosophical reserve, so distinguishable in our countrymen. They are extremely fond of jovial company; and if they did not too often sacrifice to Bacchus the joys of a vacant hour, they would be the most entertaining people in Europe: but the goodness of their wine, and the severity of their climate, are indeed some excuse for them. In other pleasures they are rather temperate, careful, and parsimonious, though avarice is seldom known amongst them; nor is any vice carried to a great excess. Their pride, which is not little, makes them too much prejudiced in favour of their country, and one another. They are neither deficient in judgment, or memory; they possess design and craft, though no deep penetration;

and

and are honest, and courageous. As to temper; active, and enthusiastic in business, persevering, and liberal, affable, and familiar; and, notwithstanding a roughness in their outward deportment, they are peculiarly possessed of the art of persuasion. They spend most of their time in reading, study, and thinking; and you find few of the common people very illiterate, though the first of their *literati* are no great scholars. They have little invention; and are no poets. Wit and humour are not known; and it rarely happens that a Scotchman laughs at ridicule. The men in general, in their persons, are large and disproportioned, with unfavourable, long, and saturnine countenances, which, perhaps, are encouraged by their education, and their seldom exerting their risible muscles. But, I think, there never was a nation, whose faces shewed their character more strongly marked, or physiognomies, from whose lineaments you might so easily guess their internal conceptions. The women are more to be admired than the men, and when young, are very beautiful: but the bloom of young desire lasts but for a day; the flower is no sooner expanded, than it begins to wither, and often dies long before its season of coming to maturity. You rarely find a woman above twenty tolerably inviting: but all under that age have a certain proportion of *embonpoint* and voluptuousness, which makes them highly the objects of luxurious love. After a particular time they grow large and lusty, which gives their features and shape, a coarse and masculine appearance. The beauty of the women of this country seems to bear the same proportion to the beauty of the women in ours, that Scotch literature does to that of South Britain. Here all the young women are handsome, but none that would be chosen by a Guido or a Titian: here none of the men are without some learning, but you rarely meet with a great and deep scholar. The disposition of the women is much inclined to sociability: they are free, affable, modest, and polite; fond of admiration, and flattery, and pleasure: no enemies to the joys of Venus, whose divinity they worship, to whom they liberally sacrifice; and, in spite of the coldness of their atmosphere

and

and northern blasts, light up as consuming fires in the hearts of their admirers, as the dames of Italy.

But the virtue which is peculiarly characteristic of the Scotch nation, is Hospitality. In this they excel every country in Europe: both the men and the women equally share in it; and indeed vie with each other in shewing politeness and humanity to strangers. When once you are acquainted with a family, you are made part of it, and they are not pleased unless you think yourself so. But as all other good qualities are frequently imposed on by ignorant, ill-designing persons; so this shares the common destiny; and the Scotch often rue the hour that they bestowed civilities on objects, who are unworthy, and insensible of their kindness. I am afraid they frequently meet with the fate of Sir John Brute, and get no other recompence for eating their meat, and drinking their drink, than this answer, "*that their adversary wears a sword:*" it being too often the case that they have been deceived by persons pretending to their good offices, and assuming false characters. This has produced an inquisitiveness concerning the family and circumstances of those they entertain, which they carry to an excess; and are not contented with a general knowledge of their connections and friends, but wish to be informed of every minute and trifling circumstance relating to them. At first this seems odd and ridiculous to a stranger; especially as it has the appearance of making a comparison with themselves; for they are sure to interlard their interrogatories with stories respecting their own genealogies, and antiquity, or nobility of their families; of which they are extremely fond, and often too sanguine in their commendations: this indeed seems to be a national defect. But we are all of us blind to our own failings: the continual commerce we have with our inclinations disguises them to us: our reason contracts a kind of familiarity with our faults, when at the same time it weighs, examines, and condemns those of our neighbours.

It is impossible at Edinburgh to be concealed or unknown: for though you enter into the City a mere traveller, and unacquainted, you cannot be there many hours before you are watched, and your name,

name, and place of abode, found out by the Cadies. These are a Society of men who constantly attend the Cross in the High-street, and whose office it is to do any thing that any body can want, and discharge any kind of business. On this account it is necessary for them to make themselves acquainted with the residence and negotiation of all the inhabitants; and they are of great utility, as without them it would be very difficult to find any body, on account of the great height of the houses, and the number of families in every building. This Society is under particular regulations, and it requires some interest to become a member of it. It is numerous, and contains persons for every use and employment, who faithfully execute all commands at a very reasonable price. Whether you stand in need of a *valet de place*, a pimp, a thief-catcher, or a bully, your best resource is to the fraternity of Cadies. In short, they are the tutelary guardians of the City; and it is intirely owing to them, that there are fewer robberies, and less house-breaking in Edinburgh, than any where else.—But I have filled my paper, and must take my leave of you;

you; being well assured that I need give you no further reason for my remaining here, than a description of its inhabitants. In a country where a man can find every thing he can wish, from the enjoyments of society, why should he not be contented? For me, I am happy at present; and when I find myself otherwise, it will then be time enough to enquire

> Quæ tellus sit lenta gelu, quæ putris ab æstu,
> Ventus in Italiam, quis bene vela ferat.

Adieu.

Your's sincerely.

LETTER XII.

An Account of the public and private Diversions of the Inhabitants of Edinburgh; and Manner of educating the young Ladies.

To Miss Elizabeth R ⸺

Edinburgh, December 30, 1774.

AS a letter from my dear Miss R ⸺ is always accompanied with the greatest pleasure, your last did not stand in need of the good news it contained, to render it more agreeable. I sincerely wish you much amusement during your residence in London; but, I must say, I envy the happiness of those gallants who are to enjoy the satisfaction of your company:

> To sit and see thee all the while,
> Softly speak, and sweetly smile.

For my own part, I must content myself with the entertainments this country affords; which, let me tell you, are by no means contemptible, whatever opinion you may entertain

tain of them. We have an elegant Playhouse, and tolerable performers; assemblies, concerts, public gardens, and walks, card parties, and a hundred other diversions, which in some degree keep me from pining for your Festino, Bach's concert, or Almack's.

As the genius of any people is not more easily discovered in their serious moments, than when they give a loose to freedom and pleasure: so the Scotch nation is peculiarly characterised by the mode of their diversions. A sober sedate elegance pervades them all, blended with an ease and propriety which delights, and is sure to meet with approbation. A Scotchman does not relax himself for amusements, as if to pass away the hour: he seems, even in the height of pleasure, busy and intent, and as he would do, were he about to gain some advantage. His diversions are not calculated to seduce the unwary, or recreate the idle, but to unbend the mind, without corrupting it. He seems as if in his infancy he had been taught to make learning his diversion, and was now reversing it, and making his diversion his study. But besides the public entertainments of this City, which are

derived

derived from company, the inhabitants have more resources of pleasure within themselves, than in many other places. The young people paint, draw, are fond of music, or employ their hours in reading, and acquiring the accomplishments of the mind. Every boarding-school Miss has something of this kind to recommend her, and make her an agreeable companion: and, instead of a little smattering of French, which is the highest ambition to attain in Queen Square, you find them in Edinburgh entertaining in conversation, sentimental, and well-informed. The mode of education of the young ladies, is here highly to be commended, and admirably calculated to make them good wives. Besides needle-work, and those trifling arts, which are the principal of their instruction in England, the precepts of morality, virtue, and honour, are taught them from their earliest infancy, whilst they are instructed to consider themselves as beings born for society, for more than outside appearance, and transitory pleasure, and to attend to the knowledge of what is useful, rather than the œconomy of a Tambour-frame. The ladies also who undertake this arduous task,

task of instruction, are persons much better qualified in general than in other countries. They likewise introduce them into the politest company, and give them a taste for elegant and proper amusements; that, when they leave school, they are not only mistresses of those accomplishments which are necessary to command a family, but have the deportment and behaviour of experienced women of fashion. No ladies in Scotland ever murder the precious moments in what is called " work," which is neither entertainment or profit, merely because they must have the appearance of doing something, whilst they see every one employed around them. They let no minute escape without its respective office, which may be of utility to themselves or others; and, after a proper sacrifice to reading and literature, gain instruction from society and conversation. I have often thought it a principal defect in the education of the English ladies, that they are taught to pay so much attention to the practice of sewing work, and other needle operations, whilst they neglect learning of greater importance and pleasure. Since they have minds equally
capable

capable of inſtruction with the other ſex, why ſhould they not be enlightened with the ſame kind of knowledge? eſpecially as they ſeem more ſuited to it, as well from their ſuperior ſenſibility, as their greater leiſure and domeſtic life. Why ſhould the characteriſtic which diſtinguiſhes us from brutes, be ſo ſtrongly cultivated in the male, and have ſo little attention paid to it in the female ſpecies? Wiſdom and ſcience are not perfections in us merely becauſe we are men, but as reaſonable creatures, who have the pre-eminence over the reſt of the creation. It is indeed neceſſary for the ladies to know theſe things, in order to qualify them for domeſtic œconomy; but I have no idea of any woman, except her whoſe circumſtances cannot afford the expence of paying a ſervant, making them her employ, or putting them in practice.

The married ladies of this City ſeldom entertain large ſets of company, or have routs, as in London: They give the preference to private parties, and *converſaziones*, where they play at cards for ſmall ſums,

sums, and never run the risk of being obliged to discharge a debt of honour at the expence of their virtue and innocence. They often frequent the theatre, and shew great taste and judgment in the choice of plays where Mr. Digges performs a principal character.

As to exercise, they seldom ride on horseback; but find much pleasure in walking, to which the soil and country is peculiarly adapted, being dry, pleasant, and abounding in prospects, and romantic scenes. It is likewise customary for them to drive in their carriages to the sands at Leith and Musselburgh, and parade backwards and forwards, after the manner of Scarborough, and other public places of sea-bathing resort. For vivacity and agility in dancing, none excel the Scotch ladies: their execution in reels and country-dances is amazing; and the variety of steps which they introduce, and the justness of their ear is beyond description. They are very fond also of minuets, but fall greatly short in the performance of them, as they are deficient in grace and elegance in their motions.

motions. Many of them play on the harpsicord and guittar, and some have music in their voices: though they rather love to hear others perform than play themselves.

I do not think the Scotch ladies are great proficients in the languages. They rarely attempt any thing further than the French; which, indeed, they speak with great propriety, fluency, and good accent; but they make up for it by their accurate and just knowledge of their own. They talk very grammatically; are peculiarly attentive to the conformity of their words to their ideas, and are great critics in the English tongue. They chiefly read history, and plaintive poetry: but elegies and pastorals are their favourites. Novels and romances they feel, and admire; and those chiefly which are tender, sympathetic, soothing, or melancholy. Their hearts are soft and full of passion, and a well-told story makes a deep impression on them. Like virgin wax, a gentle heat mollifies their minds, which reflects the finest touches of art and sentiment. —Nor are the gentlemen in Edinburgh less

less rational in their diversions than the ladies. There is only one, in which I can censure their conduct: they rather pay too much respect to the divinity of Bacchus, and offer too copious libations at the shrine of that jovial deity. Their wines, indeed, of all kinds, are excellent, and their climate not the most comfortable; so that some allowance ought to be made them in that respect. But as they are, they are by no means so intemperate as the Germans; and, perhaps, their appearing to me in the least intemperate, may be occasioned by my peculiar aversion to, and abstinence from all intoxicating liquors. I have neither taste to relish, nor head to bear them. I have no idea of a man extending the pleasure of drinking beyond thirst, or forcing, in imagination, an appetite artificial, and against nature.

The youths in this country are very manly in their exercises and amusements. Strength and agility seems to be most their attention. The insignificant pastimes of marbles, tops, &c. they are totally unacquainted with. The diversion which is peculiar

culiar to Scotland, and in which all ages find great pleasure, is golf. They play at it with a small leathern ball, like a fives ball, and a piece of wood, flat on one side, in the shape of a small bat, which is fastened at the end of a stick, of three or four feet long, at right angles to it. The art consists in striking the ball with this instrument, into a hole in the ground, in a smaller number of strokes than your adversary. This game has the superiority of cricket and tennis, in being less violent and dangerous; but in point of dexterity and amusement, by no means to be compared with them. However, I am informed that some skill and nicety are necessary to strike the ball to the proposed distance and no further, and that in this there is a considerable difference in players. It requires no great exertion and strength, and all ranks and ages play at it. They instruct their children in it, as soon as they can run alone, and grey hairs boast their execution. As to their other diversions, they dance, play at cards, love shooting, hunting, and the pleasures of the field;

field; but are proficients in none of them. When they are young, indeed, they dance, in the manner of their country, extremely well; but afterwards (to speak in the language of the turf) they train off, and are too robust and muscular to possess either grace or agility.

I am sorry to say the hazard table is in high fashion and estimation. There are clubs in Edinburgh who may vie with White's or Almack's. But the misfortune is, there is a deficiency of ready money, which obliges them to keep books, by which they transfer their debts to one another. This renders it both inconvenient and troublesome to strangers to engage them: for, if you lose, their necessity compels them to demand immediate payment; and, on the contrary, if you chance to be succesful, they refer you to twenty different people, before you can expect your money; and you have reason to bless your stars, if ever you obtain it.—I do not know any thing so disgusting or against the grain of politeness, as being obliged to dun a gentleman for a game-debt; but here it is absolutely necessary: if you do not, you play without the least chance of being a winner.

And now, my dear Miss R —— I must take my leave of you, wishing you to believe me

    your ever sincere friend,

        and much obliged, humble servant.

LETTER XIII.

On the Theatre.

To R. D. Esq.

Edinburgh, January 2, 1775.

SIR,

EDINBURGH, which has been for a long time without trade or company, a mere mass without spirits, seems to be animated with new life. The classes in the College are sitting, the terms are begun, the scenes of diversion are opened, and all is business, pleasure, and confusion.

This metropolis is said to be very gay; and, if I may judge from the little specimen I have already had of it, reports say nothing but the truth. The concerts have received the assistance of a new singer from London, the assemblies are opened for the reception of those who choose to dance, and the theatrical heroes have already opened their campaign. As yet, I believe, they have had but few spectators, as the genteel people here fix one day

day for beginning to partake of these amusements, and are so very polite, that they never go before that day on any account. In compliance with your desire, I take this leisure of acquainting you with the present state of the Theatre, and the performances there.

The present Theatre is situated at the end of the New Bridge in the New Town, and on the outside is a plain structure like most others of the same nature. It was built by the subscription of a certain number of gentlemen, who let it originally to a manager for four hundred pounds a year. Mr. Ross was the first person who took it, and his name was inserted in the patent, which made him manager as long as he chose. A few years ago, plays were not in that repute at Edinburgh they now are. The ministers, zealous for the good of their flock, preached against them, and the poor players were entirely routed: they have now, however, once more taken the field, and the clergy leave them to their ungodliness. During these contests, Mr. Ross found, that the benefits of the theatre did not answer to the expences of it, and retreated in good time. Our modern Aristo-

Ariftophanes, who imagined he had wit enough to laugh the Scotch out of their money, took it of Mr. Rofs at the fame price that was originally paid for it. He brought on all his own comedies fuccefsively; but as moft of the humour was local and particular, few people here underftood it. Now and then, indeed, a very civil gentleman was fo kind as to explain what he had been told in London, fuch a joke alluded to; but as jokes always lofe their ftrength in travelling, nobody was the wifer for the explanation. But when, in the courfe of acting, Mr. Foote attempted to introduce the Minor upon the ftage, the minifters, who had long lain dormant, now rofe up in arms. The character of Mrs. Cole gave them offence. They imagined themfelves pointed out; but were fo kind as to throw the injury upon religion. They acted juft upon the fame principles as the Monks did with Boccacio, who having told many ridiculous ftories of their gluttony, and their amours in his Decameron, they very wifely agreed, that he had faid many difrefpectful things of religion in general.

The

The Scotch Clergy, not contented with damning the play itself, very piously pronounced all those damned who went to see it. Parties, however, rose on this occasion; and many were so wicked as to insist on its being performed. Riots ensued: the unrighteous triumphed, and the poor play was performed.

Mr. Foote, however, found, that to gain half the Town was not sufficient; the whole of it was necessary for his business; and therefore, when he perceived that he could not bring them into good humour, it was his duty to retire. However, on leaving Edinburgh, he made the best of a bad bargain, and raised the rent to five hundred pounds a-year, for which sum he let it to Mr. Digges, the present manager.

The Proprietors now saw the mistake they had been guilty of, in leaving it in the power of Mr. Ross to let it out to other people, and thus, in some measure, to deprive them of their own property. If any advantageous increase of rent could have been made, they thought themselves the only persons who were entitled to it; but of this they had deprived themselves, and put the house on a worse footing than it was at the first; for if four hundred pounds had already been found to be too large a rent, five hundred must be still more distressing, and prevent the manager from bringing good actors to entertain the Town. However, under all these disadvantages, Mr. Digges took the Playhouse. Some little juvenile extravagancies, more than any natural turn for the Stage, induced Mr. Digges to quit the Military Profession, to which he was bred, and become an Actor. Driven from the first line he took the second; and as he could not gain admittance to the London Theatre, he became manager at Edinburgh.

When one recollects the former profession of Mr. Digges, the politeness of his manners, and his other accomplishments, one is sorry that his necessities should ever have driven him to the stage; but when one is witness to the attention he pays to his business, to his extreme excellence as an actor, and to the pleasure which he gives to his audience, at such

such moments, every man is selfish enough to be happy that those necessities made him a player.

As to himself, he derives all those brilliant qualifications from nature, which form a great actor. He has a handsome and expressive countenance, a penetrating eye, and a good voice. Some people will tell you, that there is a severity in his look, ill-suited to comic parts; but those who have seen him in the part of Macheath, must discover that he can dress it in smiles when he pleases. His person is rather above the middle size, well formed, and, as far as his time of life will allow of, capable of assuming any appearance. If he has any fault, generally considered, it is that of not walking the stage so properly as might be expected. He throws too much of that carelessness and indifference into his manner, which, in some characters, approaches to the vulgar, and can never be adapted to tragedy in any. He, however, excells so much in both, that I scarce know to which to give the preference. In some future letter I shall take the

the liberty of sending you my opinion of his merits in his different parts; at present I find I shall scarce have room for the little account which I proposed giving you of the Theatre.

The Theatre is of an oblong form, and designed after the manner of the foreign ones. I do not know its exact dimensions; but at three shillings (which is the price of admittance into the pit and boxes) it is capable of containing about one hundred and thirty pounds. The pit seems considered here as the *Parterre* in the French theatre, into which gentlemen go who are not sufficiently dressed for the boxes. On very crowded nights the ladies sometimes sit here, and then that part of it is divided by a partition. The ornaments are few, and in an unaffected plain style, which, on the whole, has a very elegant appearance. It is lighted with wax, and the scenery is well painted; though they do not excel in those *jeux de theâtre* which please and astonish the common people in London. The whole of their machinery is luckily very bad; and, therefore, much to the credit of their understandings,

understandings, they have seldom any Harlequin entertainments: I have only seen one or two since I came here; but the *deceptio visûs*, if such it could be called, was so miserable, that the poor players themselves seemed ashamed of it.

The upper galleries, or, as they obligingly term them in London, "the Gods," seem here very compassionate Divinities. You sometimes hear the murmurings of displeasure at a distance; but they never rain down oranges, apples, &c. on the heads of the unfortunate actors. They suffer them very quietly " to " strut their hour upon the stage," and if then they dislike them, " they are literally " heard no more."

It is probable, that from an attention to these small and seemingly trivial circumstances, that you discover more of the real manners of a people, than from the greater and more public events in life, where the passions are naturally excited, and men act under a disguise. A boisterous fellow in England, who thinks it a part of his privilege to do what he thinks proper, provided neither the laws nor *magna charta* forbid it, when he takes a dislike to an

actor,

actor, drives all the players off the stage, puts an end to the performance, and insults the whole audience. A Frenchman, and a Scotchman, whom an arbitrary government in one instance, and the remains of it in the other, has softened and refined, keep their quarrels to themselves, consider the poor players as incapable of resistance, and shew their dislike to them only by not applauding them.

I have the honour to be, &c.

LETTER

LETTER XIV.

Mr. Digges's Merit in Comedy.

To R. D. Esq;

Edinburgh, January 7, 1775.

SIR,

THE best Actors who have yet appeared, though long confined within the narrow limits of a strolling company, whenever they have discovered any uncommon degree of excellence, have always been brought on the London theatre; where the rewards of merit are so great, that if an actor has either avarice or ambition, he is sure some day to become eminent. Mutual excellence produces reciprocal emulation; and by a collision with other and better performers, the little asperities of provincial dialect and provincial action, are gradually worn away. From a course of proper imitation, he at length becomes the object of imitation to others, and fixes the standard from which he cannot recede. A London audience are always too observant to

permit

permit an actor to fall into that indolence which a confcioufnefs of acknowledged fuperiority too often produces.

Mr. Digges enjoyed none of thefe advantages: being denied accefs to the London theatre, he had no opportunity of forming himfelf upon what are thought to be the beft models, nor even of imitating what was acknowledged to be the example of good acting. His merits, therefore, like his genius, are all his own.—" *Juvat integros acce-* " *dere fontes*;" and, as far as I can judge, he copies in no inftance from any performer I have feen. Wherever he gives a different interpretation to any paffage, wherever new tones of voice are indulged, new action introduced; in fhort, whenever he varies from the common line, thefe beauties, if they are fuch, are all the refult of his own judgment; and if he fails, he has at leaft the negative merit of failing fingly, and does not blindly follow a multitude to do wrong.

He is now at the head of a company who feem intended as foils to himfelf; and though they change every year, I am informed they never change for the better. The fmallnefs
of

of the salaries accounts for this: there is only one or two whose pay exceeds a guinea a week; which, in a metropolis like Edinburgh, where the necessaries of life are almost as dear as in London, is scarce a subsistence; nor can the receipts of the house afford more, while the rent is so high. Mr. Digges is therefore constrained to do that from necessity, which, I am told, Mr. Garrick does from choice. Whenever the latter acts, he appoints the worst in his company, in order to appear to greater advantage himself: If this is true, it is a pitiful stratagem, and totally unworthy of the great abilities of Mr. Garrick.

As the Edinburgh company are very small as well as very bad, Mr. Digges is obliged to perform all the principal parts, and to act every night of representation, which is four times each week. From hence you may well imagine, that as he is constrained to personate such a number of different characters, it is impossible he should excel in all. Without commenting, therefore, upon those he probably may be deficient in, and in which he would not appear but from necessity, I will acquaint you with his principal parts.

Captain

Captain Macheath in *The Beggar's Opera*; Sir John Reſtleſs in *All in the Wrong*; Sir John Brute in *The Provoked Wife*; the Guardian in the Farce of that name; Pierre in *Venice preſerved*; Cardinal Wolſey in *Henry the Eighth*; and Cato; form the liſt of his moſt diſtinguiſhed characters: and in theſe, I think, he is excelled by no actor I have yet ſeen on any ſtage. The general run of actors, who have performed the part of Macheath, ſeem to imagine that a good voice was the only thing requiſite, and that the audience muſt certainly be won by power of ſinging. From this cauſe, though many of them have ſung it finely, none as yet have acted it properly. Mr. Digges, who, to a good taſte in muſic, joins a manly and clear voice, performs the ballads ſufficiently well without being drawn away by the tricks of ſounds from the meaning and expreſſion of the character. He ſtill preſerves the gay, thoughtleſs Libertine in every ſcene, daſhed with that proper degree of low humour which may be ſuppoſed a part in the character of an Highwayman: his action is moſt happily adapted

to

to the part, and enforces every thing he says; particularly in that song,

> " The first time at the looking-glass
> " The mother sets her daughter:" &c.

In singing this little air he is every thing the most critical judgment can wish for, and much more than one could possibly imagine the part would allow.

In the part of Sir John Restless, Mr. Digges discovers very capital merit. Though Mr. King of Drury-lane theatre has long been supposed the first in this part, I am now convinced that it has been granted to him without his deserving it: he degrades the character. The situations into which the jealousy of Sir John betrays him, are certainly ludicrous, but the passion itself is serious: though the causes are " trifles light as air " to others, they are not so to himself: he blunders on from mistake to mistake; one moment seeing the folly of his suspicion, and the next erring again; hurried on by a confusion of circumstances, which are never clearly unravelled till the last act: but all this is not the result of folly or buffoonery, but of feeling.

ing. Mr. Digges makes the proper distinction: he never anticipates the mirth his mistakes occasion: he never laughs before his audience; but is sensible that the real ridicule arises not from making the part absurd, but from being in earnest. The dark, gloomy suspicion of tragedy, as in Othello, leads to blood and murder; the jealousy of comedy to mirthful incidents — but they are still supposed to feel the passion.

"Interdum et vocem comœdia tollit,
"Iratusque Chremes tumido delitigat ore."

Mr. Digges's figure, his manners, his whole appearance as well as action, conspire to render him infinitely superior to any actor I have seen in this character.

Sir John Brute is esteemed Mr. Digges's *chef-d'œuvre* in comedy; and, in my opinion, he excells every actor in this part, not excepting Mr. Garrick; for I by no means subscribe to that opinion which allows our modern Roscius unequalled in every thing he undertakes: no one can deny that in general he is the best performer that ever appeared; but in some characters he certainly has been excelled.

celled. There is a conviviality, a joyousness of temper in Mr. Digges, and which is peculiarly adapted to this part, which Mr. Garrick neither has in his natural disposition, nor can he imitate it. Mr. Garrick makes poor Sir John an old superannuated Brute, and, as one would suppose, totally incapable of uttering one word of common sense: when, on the contrary, he says not only a number of sensible things, but replete with humour and good observation. In one part, however, he excells Mr. Digges,—in that where he gradually and insensibly drops asleep, the half-uttered imprecations dying away in his mouth. But Mr. Digges resumes his superiority in every other scene. At table with Lord Rake and Colonel Bully, you forget that it is an entertainment on the stage; it becomes real; and you fancy yourself not a spectator, but a guest. No man understands the ' *leges bi-bendi* ' better than Mr. Digges; and he shews them here to advantage.

When dressed in Lady Brute's cloaths he again excells Mr. Garrick: his figure, which is larger, is much more grotesque and ridiculous.

lous. When he turns himself round to the audience, after having equipped himself properly, there is not an unmoved countenance in the house: when he proposes to sweat the taylor before they make him immortal; when he is carried before the Justice; his impudent look, his dirty bedlamite appearance during the examination; and when he puts his fan before his face, and desires the Justice " to spare his blushes," the whole audience are in one continued burst of applause; which is the best and truest test of his merit. I have already seen him perform this character four separate times, and I should see him act it a fifth with equal pleasure.

I will conclude this long letter with mentioning Mr. Digges's last part in comedy, the Guardian. This *petite* piece was written by Mr. Garrick, as a ridicule on that self-sufficient race of Coxcombs, who fancy themselves irresistible, and that every woman must be in love with them. A *petit maître*, just imported from France, pays his addresses (if such they can be called) to a young Girl of fortune
lately

lately returned from a boarding-fchool to her Guardian — a man of fenfe, merit, and accomplifhments; and whofe age is drawn at forty. Infpired with a juft regard for fuch merits, fhe conceives an affection for her Guardian in fecret; which her diffidence forbids her being the firft to difclofe. The miftake is carried on for a long time; as nothing can convince the young lover, but that the lady admires him as much as he admires himfelf; and he fays, 'her eyes tell 'him fo.' But he finds himfelf miftaken: an *eclairciffement* is at laft made; and the poor Macaroni is left in the lurch. The whole tenor of it is the triumph of fenfe over folly.

Mr. Digges has on this occafion only to appear in his own character, and to give utterance to his own fentiments. Grave, manly, handfome, accomplifhed; he is in every point the character itfelf. The female eye is no longer pleafed with foppery and affectation, but acknowledges the juftice of the preference fhe has given; and that modern difgrace to manhood, that puny, motley animal, a Macaroni, a Macaroni, sinks into his original nothingness: for, as Horatio says,

> " A skipping, dancing, prating tribe ye are,
> " Fit only for yourselves; ye herd together!
> " And when the circling glass warms your vain
> " hearts,
> " Ye talk of women whom ye never saw,
> " And fancy raptures which you never felt."

In a future letter I will send you my opinion of Mr. Digges's merit in Tragedy; at present I have scarce paper sufficient to assure you how much

I am, &c,

LETTER

LETTER XV.

Mr. Digges's Merit in Tragedy.

To R. D. Esq;

Edinburgh, January 12, 1775.

SIR,

CERTAIN people here, who do not admire Mr. Digges so much as I do, will tell you, that there is a severity in his look which is highly unpleasing, and a roughness in his voice incapable of being modulated into softer and milder tones. They all, however, agree, that these circumstances seem to form him by nature for personating the part of Pierre. That gloomy resentment, that sullen ferocity, that fixed purpose of vengeance, which distinguish his character to the last moment, can only be marked by a stern countenance, and expressed by a firm tone of voice. There is something so repugnant to the spirit of forgiveness, and so shocking, even to human nature, throughout the whole of his conduct, that it requires uncommon merit in a performer to make it admired. As yet no actor ever excelled in it; so that Mr. Digges, in this part, stands unrivalled.

He is peculiarly happy in that scene where, after dwelling upon every circumstance to try the disposition of his friend Jaffier, he at last trusts him with the fatal business of the conspiracy. His look, his tone of voice, his action, are all expressive of that cautious timidity, with which a long habitude of suspicion, and a wicked knowledge of the world inspire a man who confides a secret of the last importance to the bosom of another. He speaks this address to Jaffier admirably:

> " I'll trust thee with a secret: there are spirits
> " This hour at work—But as thou art a man
> " Whom I have pick'd and chosen from the world,
> " Swear that thou wilt be true to what I utter:
> " And when I've told thee that which only Gods,
> " And men like gods are privy to, then swear
> " No chance or change shall wrest it from thy
> " bosom."

When he is brought before the Senate, as yet uncertain of what he is accused, though

Mr.

Mr. Digges's whole action shews that presence and intrepidity of mind which the character demands; you still discover he is counterfeiting a virtue which he has not. When at last Jaffier is produced, and he can no longer suppose them ignorant of his crime, that look of defiance which Mr. Digges then assumes, when he rejects the offered pardon and chooses death, when he denounces curses on the whole Senate, and wishes that " divisions may still vex their " councils," breathes the very spirit of his character, and discovers that obstinate and unconquered resolution, his author meant to draw.

In the following scene with Jaffier, Mr. Digges is equally admirable. His whole action, not less than the speeches themselves, is contrasted to that of his friend. That sullen and disdainful dignity with which he first regards him, and those degrading reproaches with which he insults his weakness, in betraying the secret he had confided to him, are all properly marked in Mr. Digges's performance.

In the last scene, all Pierre's former character is forgotten; he is no longer the " *Ira-*
" *cundus*

"*cundus, inexorabilis, acer.*"—His distresses draw a veil over his imperfections; and when he points to the scaffold already prepared for him, and asks Jaffier,

> "Is't fit a soldier, who has liv'd with honour,
> "Fought nation's quarrels, and been crown'd with
>   "conquest,
> "Be expos'd a common carcafs on a wheel?"

no breast can be insensible to his situation, or unmoved at the mournful and pathetic accent with which Mr. Digges utters this sentence.

I will not detain you with all the minutiæ of Mr. Digges's excellence in the part of Cardinal Wolsey. On the English stage, it is so seldom acted for want of proper representation, that one cannot from thence form any comparative idea of his merit. In this country, it is always said to be Mr. Digges's master-piece, and, probably, there is none in which (to use an expression of the Theatre) he better looks the character. His very attitude expresses the part. You see that fawning yet imperious carriage, that affected humility, with that real haughtiness, blended at one and the same instant. No words can convey to you his merit in the scene where the King first discovers his treachery, and, giving him the letter he had found, bids him

> "Take that and then to breakfast with what appe-
> "tite he can."

In one cast of his eye you anticipate his whole fate: you discover, without words, a great and proud man, dashed in one moment from power, wealth, and titles, to a bottomless abyss of poverty and derision. The mind wishes for nothing more—You have scarce any occasion for that fine soliloquy, to which he does equal justice.

I mention the part of Cato last, because, though it is not generally thought so, it is, in my opinion, Mr. Digges's best performance. In general, his voice is not susceptible of that feeble expression which most actors assume in the part of an old man. He gives you, however, the full force of that softness which appears as if involuntarily, of

that

that broken and interrupted accent, where the infirmities of nature baffle our resolution, and force us to weep in spite of ourselves. This is the exact character of Cato, who struggles, on every occasion, to suppress the natural affections, as if ashamed of them, in conformity to the doctrines of Stoicism. When he is told that his son Marcus did not, as he supposes, desert his post, but died in the defence of his country, covered with wounds; when he recovers from that momentary impression which the death of a son, even in such a cause, must give him, and in spite of parental affection breaks out into that noble thanksgiving, of

"Thanks to the Gods, my boy has done his duty!"

Mr. Digges's look and action beggar all description: and I appeal to every one who has seen him in this part, whether Mr. Garrick, in the meridian of his acting, ever pronounced a line better. Again, when he meets the corse of his son, borne by his fellow-soldiers, his action is equally fine. When he bids them set him down, that he may

may contemplate his wounds, while he bends over the dead body, and struggles to suppress those tears which he imagines would disgrace him; while he pronounces that beautiful eulogium which the love of his country inspires, and which is a soldier's best reward, nothing can be performed in a more masterly manner.

I have now given you the outlines of Mr. Digges's theatrical merit. I am sensible there are many other parts equally worthy observation, which I may have omitted; but you will remember, that I am sending you what struck me on representation only, and which I mark down from memory. It is amongst the few instances of my life where my expectations have not been disappointed; for, though I had been led to hope a great deal, Mr. Digges more than repaid it: and when you reflect, that his merit has entirely been the result of his own judgment; that he has never had a competitor to excite his emulation, nor any other object of ambition but that of pleasing his audience, in which he has meritoriously persevered for a number of years,

and

and sometimes without much encouragement; you will agree with me in thinking, that all I can say is but a poor tribute to his excellencies.

But lest you should begin to think, as many other good-natured people do, that writing panegyric is very stupid employment, I shall beg leave to conclude this letter.

I have the honour to be, &c.

LETTER XVI.

The Entertainments of Oyster-cellars, and Comely Gardens.

To R. D. Esq.

Edinburgh, January 15, 1775.

SIR,

YOU have so frequently run the round of all the fashionable diversions in other countries, as well as your own, and have so long imagined that gilded roofs and painted ceilings are the only scenes of festivity, that you will not easily believe there exist any other. There is, however, a species of entertainment, different indeed from yours, but which seems to give more real pleasure to the company who visit it, than either Ranelagh or the Pantheon. The votaries to this shrine of pleasure are numerous; and the manner is intirely new. As soon as the evening begins to grow late, a large party form themselves together, and march to the Temple; where, after descending a few steps for the benefit of being removed from profaner eyes, they are admitted by the good Guardian of it; who, doubtless, rejoices to see so large and well-disposed a company of worshippers. The Temple itself is very plain and humble. It knows no idle ornaments, no sculpture or painting; nor even so much as wax tapers— a few solitary candles of tallow cast a dim, religious light, very well adapted to the scene. There are many separate cells of different sizes, accommodated to the number of the religious, who attend in greater or smaller parties, as the spirit moves them. After the company have made the proper sacrifices, and staid as long as they think necessary, the utensils are removed, proper donations made to the priestess; who, like all others of her profession, is not very averse to money; and they retire in good order, and disperse for the evening.

In plain terms, this shrine of festivity is nothing more than an Oyster-cellar, and its Votaries the First People in Edinburgh. A few evenings ago I had the pleasure of being asked to one of these entertainments, by a Lady. At that time I was not acquainted with

with this scene of " high life below stairs;" and therefore, when she mentioned the word Oyster Cellar, I imagined I must have mistaken the place of invitation: she repeated it, however, and I found it was not my business to make objections; so agreed immediately. You will not think it very odd, that I should expect, from the place where the appointment was made, to have had a *partie tête-à-tête*. I thought I was bound in honour to keep it a secret, and waited with great impatience till the hour arrived. When the clock struck the hour fixed on, away I went, and enquired if the lady was there—" O " yes," cried the woman, " she has been here " an hour, or more." I had just time to curse my want of punctuality, when the door opened, and I had the pleasure of being ushered in, not to one lady, as I expected, but to a large and brilliant company of both sexes, most of whom I had the honour of being acquainted with.

The large table, round which they were seated, was covered with dishes full of oysters, and pots of porter. For a long time, I could not suppose that this was the only entertainment

ment we were to have, and I sat waiting in expectation of a repast that was never to make its appearance. This I soon found verified, as the table was cleared, and glasses introduced. The ladies were now asked whether they would choose brandy or rum punch? I thought this question an odd one, but I was soon informed by the gentleman who sat next me, that no wine was sold here; but that punch was quite " the thing." The ladies, who always love what is best, fixed upon brandy punch, and a large bowl was immediately introduced. The conversation hitherto had been insipid, and at intervals: it now became general and lively. The women, who, to do them justice, are much more entertaining than their neighbours in England, discovered a great deal of vivacity and fondness for repartee. A thousand things were hazarded, and met with applause; to which the oddity of the scene gave propriety, and which could have been produced in no other place. The general ease, with which they conducted themselves, the innocent freedom of their manners, and their unaffected good-nature,

all

all conspired to make us forget that we were regaling in a cellar; and was a convincing proof, that, let local customs operate as they may, a truly polite woman is every where the same. Bigotted as, I know you to be to more fashionable amusements, you yourself would have confessed, that there was in this little assembly more real happiness and mirth; than in all the ceremonious and splendid meetings at Soho.

When the company were tired of conversation, they began to dance reels, their favourite dance, which they performed with great agility and perseverance. One of the gentlemen, however, fell down in the most active part of it, and lamed himself; so the dance was at an end for that evening. On looking at their watches, the ladies now found it was time to retire; the coaches were therefore called, and away they went, and with them all our mirth.

The company, which were now reduced to a party of gentlemen, began to grow very argumentative, and consequently very dull. Pipes and politics were introduced; but as I found we were not likely " *ex fumo dare* " *lucem,*"

"*lucem*," I took my hat, and wished them a good night. The bill for entertaining half a dozen very fashionable women, amounted only to two shillings a-piece. If you will not allow the entertainment an elegant one, you must at least confess that it is cheap.

And now, Sir, I beg that you will treat these Oyster Cellars with respect, and consider them, for the future, as very genteel meetings. The Beauties of this place, who frequent them, ought to keep them sacred from your reproach; for they are mysteries of their own. Not many years ago, you will remember a certain nightly meeting in London, commonly distinguished by the name of Mother Midnight's, which was constantly crowded with the most fashionable people of both sexes: a meeting equally distinguished for its seasonable hours, and the utility of its entertainment: for what could be more improving, than making a turkey dance, merely by putting a small quantity of red hot iron under its feet? Or teaching a few refractory cats to squall a concert? The design was indeed patriotic, and calculated to save to England

England those immense sums which have since been bestowed on French dancers and Italian singers; and which, in that case, would have been confined to the merits of our own countrymen.

The Oyster Cellars of Edinburgh, however, are exempt from one charge, with which those of London were accused, and not without reason: there are no intrigues carried on here. The privacy of the scene, and the numbers that frequent them, may indeed give cause for suspicion; but I believe it is a groundless one. No lady has as yet removed from them into the Commissary Court; a little apartment, where three or four "ex-" "cellent young men," (as Shylock says) sit in judgment over the infidelities of wives: and who, when they see any ladies very much tired of their husbands, are so kind as to oblige them with a separation.

You will find, that the Oyster Cellar is only a winter entertainment. In summer, another kind takes place. This is an humble and very distant imitation of Marybone Gardens, and is held in a place called Comely Garden;

dens; not that they have any relation to the name; for there is not the leaft beauty about them. They are open twice a-week, from the beginning of June till the latter end of Auguft, and the admittance is only one fhilling.

Having nothing to do one evening, at the end of laft fummer, I went there with an intention of feeing what was to be feen. I walked up and down the Gardens, but nobody appeared. I then approached the orcheftra, which was the ruins of an old pidgeon houfe, with no other alteration but that of removing the pigeons, and making room for four or five muficians, who were playing a compofition, moft mufical, moft melancholy, out of one of the windows. They continued this fome time; but finding there was no one to liften to them, and that " they were waft-" ing their fweetnefs on the defert air," they gave over playing, and retired for the evening.

I now find, that thefe Gardens are confidered by the fafhionable people here, as a very unfafhionable place, and only frequented
by

by the *Burgeois*. It is possible, that even this place, under the direction of a man of taste, with proper improvements, might, in some measure, resemble the public gardens in London. But the rage of diversions is here so much more moderated, and they have in general so little ready money to throw away upon articles of amusement, especially as the better sort of people are in the country at this season of the year, that I am persuaded they will never have any imitation of Vauxhall at Edinburgh. The climate would be no obstruction during the summer season, as they walk out at all hours in the evening without the least inconvenience. But the greatest objection is, that it has been thought unfashionable; and when that is the case, it is effectually condemned for ever. No place under the sun is more absolutely under the dominion of the word Fashion. If a few select people here choose to say, that such a thing is *vulgar*, there is no further questions; but it becomes so immediately.

This idea is so strong in this country, that I am persuaded, had a certain very ingenious Lord* here, who took it into his head to inform mankind they were originally born with tails, got but six other men equally as daring and ingenious to support his opinion, that, in a very short time, every man in this country would have felt for his tail on coming into a room.

I have the honour to be, &c.

* Lord M—s—do.

LETTER XVII.

On the Reception of Dr. Johnson's Tour at Edinburgh.

To R. D. Esq.

SIR, Edinburgh, January 24, 1775.

DR. Johnson's account of his tour into Scotland has just made its appearance here; and has put the country into a flame. Every body finds some reason to be affronted. A thousand people, who know not a single creature in the Western isles, interest themselves in their cause, and 'are offended at the accounts that are given of them. But let this unfortunate writer say what he will, it must be confessed they return it with interest: Newspapers, magazines, pamphlets, all teem with abuse of the Doctor: while one day some very ingenious criticisms shew how he might have wrote such a thing better; the next, others equally ingenious prove, that he had better never have wrote such a thing at all. In this general uproar, amidst this

strife

strife of tongues, it is impossible that a dispassionate man should be heard; so I sit down a quiet spectator of what passes, and enjoy the storm in tranquillity.

Though I cannot say I am a friend to this method of revenge, or to seeing these great men descend to abuse one another, like mere common mortals, I must confess, at the same time, that Dr. Johnson has deserved the treatment he meets with. He was received with the most flattering marks of civility by every one; and his name had opened to him an acquaintance, which his most sanguine wishes could scarce have hoped for; but which his manners would certainly never have obtained. He was indeed looked upon as a kind of miracle in this country; and almost carried about for a shew. Every one desired to have a peep at this Phenomenon; and those who were so happy as to be in his company, were silent the moment he spoke, lest they should interrupt him, and lose any of the good things he was going to say. It was expected that he should speak by inspiration. But the Doctor, who never said any thing that did not

not convey some gross reflection upon themselves, soon made them sick of jokes which were at their own expence. Indeed, from all the accounts I have been able to learn, he repaid all their attention to him with ill-breeding; and when in the company of the ablest men in this country, and who are certainly his superiors in point of abilities, his whole design was to shew them how contemptibly he thought of them. But those, who make Gods, and then fall down and worship them, should not be disappointed at the stupidity of their own idols. The Scotch, who looked up to Dr. Johnson as something supernatural, should not have been surprised at finding him quite the reverse. Admiration and acquaintance, you know, are generally said to be incompatible: with him, they must always be so: he has neither the ambition to desire, nor the manners to engage, attention. Had the Scotch been more acquainted with Dr. Johnson's private character, they would have expected nothing better. A man of illiberal manners and surly disposition, who all his life long had been at enmity with the Scotch,

takes

takes a sudden resolution of travelling amongst them; not, according to his own account, " to find a people of liberal and refined edu-" cation, but to see wild men and wild man-" ners." Confined to one place, and accustomed to one train of ideas; incapable of acquiescing in all the different tempers he might meet with; and mingling with different societies, he descends from his study, where he had spent his whole life, to see the world in the Highlands, and Western Isles of Scotland. Behold this extraordinary man on his journey, in quest of barbarism! and at length sitting down, wearied, and discontented, because he has met with some degree of civility in the most desert parts; or, to speak more properly, because he has found nothing more barbarous than himself.

Poor Johnson, who, probably, had never travelled more than a few miles from London, before he came there, must naturally be astonished at every thing he saw, and would dwell upon every common occurrence as a wonder. One cannot, therefore, be surprised at his observing ' that the windows in some
' of

' of the little hovels in Scotland, do not
' draw up, as his own do in London; or that
' such a spot of ground does not produce
' grass, but is very fertile in thistles.' He
found himself in a new world: his sensations
were those of a child just brought forth into
day-light; whose organs are confused with
the numerous objects that surround him; and
who discovers his surprise at every thing he
sees. Men of the world would not have descended
to such remarks. A petty and frivolous
detail of trifling circumstances are the
certain signs of ignorance or inexperience.
The Scotch should have treated them in this
manner, and disregarded them. For my own
part, to say the best of it, I look upon all
his observations in regard to men and manners,
to be those of a man totally unacquainted
with mankind.

Most of his information, I know to have
been received from the meanest and most ignorant
of the people. During his stay at St.
Andrew's, he resided in the house of a Professor
of that University, a very ingenious man, and
capable of giving him all the information he
could have wished; but he never enquired

one

one word about the matter: and yet, after this, does Dr. Johnson sit down, and give you a long, circumstantial account of St. Andrew's, with scarce three words of truth in the whole of it. But this might be forgiven. In regard, however, to facts, to conversation, and to affairs of literature, one might reasonably have expected from the Doctor more candour, and more veracity. But here again we are to be disappointed: he has his own maxims, and he never moves from them. He had taken a resolution not to believe Fingal to be the work of Ossian, but an imposition on the public by Mr. Macpherson: and, after various observations almost unintelligible from the language they are conveyed in, he is so kind as to say, " I
" asked a very learned Minister in the Isle of
" Sky, (who had used all arts to make me be-
" lieve the genuineness of the book) whether
" at last, he believed it himself? But he
" would not answer: he wished me to be de-
" ceived for the honour of his countrymen;
" but would not directly and formally de-
" ceive me. Yet has this man's testimony
" been produced publicly as of one who held

" Fingal

" Fingal to be the work of Offian." This is a plain, simple tale, that I own staggered me: I have only to regret for the Doctor's sake, that not one word of it is true. " Of all the lies in the catalogue," as Touchstone says, " one ought to be most cautious " of giving the lie direct:" in some cases it is unfortunately necessary. In a conversation with the Laird of Macleod, who was present at the time, and whose word, I am bold to say, I can depend upon, I asked him whether this was the truth or not ? his reply was this, " Quite the contrary, I assure you : Doctor " Johnson was very overbearing, and laugh-" ed at the Minister for giving credit to such " an imposition. At last he asked him, " whether he seriously did believe it ? the " gentleman's answer was, that he did."

Now what degree of attention ought one to pay to a man who can misrepresent facts so grossly, and interpret them to his own purposes ? " A Scotchman," Dr. Johnson says, " must be a very sturdy moralist, who does " not love Scotland better than truth :" But what country or what attachment is it that
makes

makes the Doctor himself regard truth so little?

On many other subjects his observations are equally ingenious, novel, and entertaining. In spite of the many able men this country has produced, and whose works are an honour to every part of science, the Doctor finds out the Scotch are no scholars, but that they possess a middle state betwixt profound learning and profound ignorance. Thus you see how we have been hitherto imposed upon. Some people have thought that Dr. Robertson, Mr. Hume, and Dr. Beattie, were ingenious men: but quite the contrary; they are only a few degrees above profound ignorance. Suppose one should ask, At what line of this literary barometer the Doctor places himself? whether it is at profound knowledge, at perfection itself, or whether he is contented with only being a little above Mr. Hume, or even Dr. Beattie? How much are the world obliged to Dr. Johnson, for rectifying the wrong opinion they entertained of the Scotch nation! They have, however, one consolation in all this dearth of learning, that they have no pedantry;

dantry; that they never brandish their knowledge in your face, but keep it contentedly in their pockets; that they express themselves in a natural, plain way, and to the best of their abilities; that they seek for no distinctions in words, nor pride themselves upon phrases; that they are not fond of those pompous descriptions, which " amaze the un-" learned, and make the learned smile;" but content themselves with that humble road which the mediocrity of their understandings points out to them; happy in giving no offence but to the learned Dr. Johnson, who visits them for the benefit of their ignorance, and insults them with his superiority.

   I have the honour to be, &c.

LETTER XVIII.

On the Disorder of the Country; the Infrequency of it, &c.— The Sibbins; and Cleanliness of the Inhabitants of Edinburgh.

To the Honourable William S——, Esq.

Edinburgh, January 28, 1775.

DEAR SIR,

AS I know you will pardon my thinking you, like the multitude of my own countrymen, not a little prejudiced against the natives of this country; especially as you have given me sufficient reason, by the enquiries you made in your last letter; I take the liberty of filling this sheet with endeavouring to divest you of your ill opinion, by giving you a single example, with regard to which there seems to be a general mistake; namely, the universality throughout this kingdom of that most troublesome of all disorders, called the Itch. On account of which notion, I make no doubt, but that you were

much

much furprifed to find fuch a cuftom prevailed here, as ftrangers conftantly faluting them on introduction; which was the fubject of a former letter. I affure you, on the credit of a man of honour, which I always wifh to poffefs in your efteem, inftances of it are fo rare, at leaft in this part of the country, that I really think you ftand lefs chance of catching it, than in moft parts of England. It muft be granted indeed, that in the Highlands the common people are extremely poor and neceffitous, and perhaps uncleanly in a high degree; but I really believe even there the Itch is not fo frequent as we are apt to imagine. The quantity of oatmeal which they eat, will naturally produce an eruption on the fkin, which, perhaps, much refembles that complaint, but is not of that difagreeable nature to be communicated by contact. I remember, about four years ago, I was alarmed with an appearance of this fort on my hands, owing to being accuftomed to wafh them in oatmeal and water. My ignorance, for a little while, inclined me to imagine it was the itch; but finding the fymptoms on no other part of my body, and being well assured that I had had communication with nobody that could have infected me, I was led to think that it was occasioned by something which had been applied to my hands; and accordingly I left off making use of washing them in any thing, except soap occasionally, and have never since been troubled in the same manner.

I am perfectly sensible, had this disorder been infectious, that it would have been impossible for many of the family where I then lived to have escaped; for I was so positive that it was not the itch, that I took no means of preventing it. That this is frequently the case in this country I am well assured, both from the quantity of oatmeal which the common people daily eat, and which makes a chief part of their subsistence; and from the pernicious effects which would be produced from their neglect, was it absolutely the itch.

It is well known to the physical world, that the true itch, which I believe proceeds rather from nastiness, than from foulness of blood, is of so malevolent a complexion, that, without

out any topical application to stop its progress, the *animalcula* would increase in such an abundance, that they would consume a man in a few years: but in the Highlands they are so little afraid of this *morbus avenaceus*, that it is almost essential to the very being of a Highlander; and though they take no means of prevention, it never reaches such a pitch as to destroy them, or be of dangerous consequence.

But there is a disorder which is known in this country by the name of *The Sibbins*, which is of a nature most formidable and horrid; and resembles the Yaws, which is common among the Slaves in the West Indies. The poor unhappy beings who are thus tormented, are by degrees wasted away, and eaten up by pestilential sores, and are so exceedingly offensive, that they are deprived of every assistance from their fellow-creatures. Notwithstanding the great excellence of the Esculapian art, which flourishes in this City more than in any part of Europe, it still baffles the power of medicine, and is deemed incurable.

I once

I once had a sight of a boy in this wretched situation; who presented a spectacle truly terrible and shocking. He was totally deprived of one side, which was mangled to a skeleton, whilst the other seemed just to have fallen a prey to the fury of its ravenous appetite: the distinction of features in his face was almost obliterated; his mouth and nose were one entire chasm; and his lifeless eye-ball hung staring in the socket, which seemed hollowed out, and too large to confine it: in short, he appeared a walking lazar-house.

There is also another error, which in England we are very liable to fall into, concerning the natives of this country; (equally ridiculous, and without truth, as the prevalency of the itch, and seems from thence to have taken its rise) which is, that they are extremely neglectful of Cleanliness, both in their persons and houses. With regard to the higher rank of persons, I think, in this respect, there is no judging by them, as they are nearly the same in all great and civilized places; which is the case also of the lowest dregs, who cannot but be otherwise in poverty,

verty, neceffity, and wretchedneſs. It is, therefore, from the middle claſs I ſhould form my opinion; who, as the greateſt part of any nation, bear the ſtamp and marks which are characteriſtical of it. And I cannot but ſay, that both as to themſelves and families, they pay much greater attention to neatneſs than the French, whom, in their reſemblance in this particular, they far excell.

In Edinburgh, from the unfavourable ſituation of the houſes, it is amazing the inhabitants preſerve any degree of decency; but you rarely find, in the worſt part of the Town, an obſcure lodging that has not ſome degree of neatneſs, and a certain ſimplicity about it, to make it comfortable; though I know many people would ſay, that it is impoſſible to affirm this, as in general they are ſo dark, that you cannot vouch for any thing but their obſcurity.

I am informed that Edinburgh is greatly improved in this reſpect within a few years, occaſioned by the diligence and management of the Police; which ſet an example, by being particularly careful of the cleanneſs of the ſtreets, into which, as a common ſewer, all the nuſances of the houſes are emptied at a ſtated time in the night, on the ringing of a bell, and immediately removed by perſons appointed for that purpoſe; and at the ſame time the reſervoirs being ſet open, which are placed at certain intervals in the ſtreets, carry every thing away; ſo that in the morning the ſtreets are ſo clean, that foot paſſengers walk in the middle of them. It is likewiſe a ſevere penalty to throw any thing out of the windows. But I cannot help obſerving the intolerable ſtench that is produced at this ſeaſon of the night, on the moving the tub of naſtineſs from each floor: ſuch a concatenation of ſmells I never before was ſenſible of; it has been ſometimes ſo powerful as to wake me, and prevent my ſleeping till it was ſomewhat pacified.

As I know you pay great credit to Dr. Johnſon, I will conclude with informing you that his obſervation on the windows in the City of Edinburgh, is as falſe as it is abſurd: To be ſure, in all large places, where there is a number of bad houſes, there cannot be all thoſe conveniences which pleaſure or luxury has contrived; but for the Doctor to affirm,

‘ that

'that there are no windows hung by pullies in the Old City of Edinburgh,' is almoſt too groſs a miſtake to require a contradiction. I imagine he found the windows, as he deſcribes them, in the lodgings of his intimate friend, and from thence concludes that they are in the ſame manner throughout the City. I cannot but add, that many other parts of his book deſerve the like attention. Beware, therefore, of the credit you pay to the writings of an author, who makes remarks

" by way of filling,
" To raiſe the volume price one ſhilling."

And believe me to be

  Your ever affectionate friend,

    and obliged, humble ſervant.

LETTER

LETTER XIX.

On the Cookery in Scotland; and some particular Dishes.

To S. W—— Esq;

Edinburgh, February 3, 1775.

MY GOOD FRIEND,

I Know of no word that is made use of by the generality of mankind with so little meaning, as the word *Taste*. Every one talks of *Taste*, or *the Taste*, or *the good Taste*; but few affix any idea to the term; for they do not mean their own natural Taste, but that of some body, or some set of people, or some country, which is always uncertain, always varying, and imaginary; and, in short, of which they can give no account. But this *ignis fatuus* is not oftener talked of, than followed, without being understood, perhaps to the utter ruin and destruction of the poor misguided persons who have folly or vanity enough to pursue it.

We

We find, every day, some that have lost their fortunes, because it was *the Taste* to play at hazard. Others, who have exhausted their hereditary estate, in *cameo*'s, *intaglio*'s, *antiquo*'s, and *moderno*'s, in pictures, statues, and medals, in order to acquire it. Some that have built houses which they could not live in, to conform to it; and others, who have pulled houses down, which had been the delight of their ancestors for many a generation, because they did not agree with *the modern Taste*. They listen with disgust to an Italian musician, whom they pretend to attend to with enthusiasm and rapture; and yawn in private over a sentimental comedy, which they hear with applause and admiration, because it is *the Taste*. But the greatest absurdity is, that Taste, in its proper signification, viz. the sensation of the palate, now-a-days, entirely gives place to this artificial one; and the privilege of tasting for one's self, which is a natural prerogative of nature, must be yielded up, if you wish to be admitted into the politest company. A man must dine on a ragout or fricassee, because it is
approved

approved of by a set of good eaters, or the *ſçavoir vivre*, though he is longing all the while to testify his real taste, by a frequent application to the side board and roast beef. Besides, the greatest misfortune attending it is, that this Taste is perpetually changing, and in a constant state of fluctuation; that you have no sooner acquired the proper relish, or perhaps got the better of your antipathy, than you are obliged to despise what you have been labouring at, to the great detriment and mortification of your constitution and stomach, and compelled to gratify your appetite according to a new *Taste*.

I was led into these reflections by a dinner from which I am just come, and from which I rose up almost famished with hunger, and tantalized to death by the enjoyment of other people; because my friend must needs entertain with dishes in the *highest Taste*; and, what was worse, entirely in the Scotch taste, whose cookery I cannot commend so much as their politeness and hospitality. As he is a true native of the North,

and

and very zealous for the honour of his country, and every thing that relates to it, it was impossible for me not to like a mixture, which had met with the highest approbation at Fortune's *, had been applauded to the skies by my Lord Kelly, and other celebrated knights of the trencher: and I could not but relish, what I could not swallow, because it had received the sanction of the whole kingdom of Scotland. This was a *Hagis*; a dish not more remarkable or more disgusting to the palate, than in appearance. When I first cast my eye on it, I thought it resembled a bullock's paunch, which you often meet in the streets of London in a wheel-barrow; and, on a nearer inspection, I found it really to be the stomach of a sheep, stuffed till it was as full as a foot-ball. An incision being made in the side of it, the entrails burst forth, " *ceu rapidus montano flumine torrens,*" and presented such a display of oatmeal, and sheep's liver, and

---

* The name of a man who keeps a celebrated tavern in Edinburgh.

lights, with a mofeta that accompanied them, that I could fcarcely help thinking myfelf in the *Grotto del Cane*. As I mentioned, my politenefs got the better of my delicacy, and I was prevailed on to tafte it; but I could go no farther: and, after a few encomiums on its being tender and favory, which I thought fufficient to fhew that I was not wholly deftitute of *Tafte*, I turned a hungry face towards a large tureene in the middle, which the mafter of the feaft called Cocky-leaky; and, with the greateft appearance of luxury and glee in his countenance, extracted from a quantity of broth, in which it had been boiled with leeks, a large cock, which I dare fay had been the herald of the morn for many a year. This, he exclaimed, would be exquifite, if the cook had taken care that the broth was fufficiently feafoned; and after he had tafted it, he declared that it exceeded his higheft expectations. During this time, I found fome of the company pay great attention; and, on the verdict being given, feemed rather impatient: but as I was a ftranger, and had

had not blessed my appetite with a considerable degree of Hagis, my plate was filled first, and I began upon it, whilst their eyes were all fixed on me to hear me pronounce the sentence; which I did, indeed, in the words of the verdict, but with some reluctance; for it was so hard and tough, that it seemed to require the stomach of an ostrich to digest it: and I could not help thinking, that it would have cut a much better figure in a main than on a table, as I would have defied the best warrior cock that ever came victorious from the pit of battle, to have produced a breast more impenetrable, or a leg better fortified with spurs and sinew. But " it was admirable, it was *the Taste*;" that was sufficient. The Scotchmen devoured it unmercifully, and the ladies enjoyed the broth.

I was next solicited to eat some Sheep's head, which had raised my curiosity for some time to find out what it was; and on being told, I concluded it was the head of a black sheep, and, perhaps, on that account, a rarity; for its appearance was so *sombre*, that otherwise it must have been dressed dreffed in the fmoak-jack. My being unwilling to be difappointed again, prevented my having refolution to venture on it: in order therefore to fill up the vacant interim, till a Solan Goofe, which had been the caufe of the invitation, fhould make its *entrée*, I enquired of my neighbour the manner of dreffing this fheep's head; and, on account of his clofe attachment to his plate, it was with difficulty I fqueezed from him, in halfeaten words, that it was nothing but a plainboiled, common fheep's head with the fkin on, from which the wool had been finged, which was the caufe of its dark complexion.

But behold the Goofe! The Hagis had been in *Tafte*, the Cocky-leeky had been in *the Tafte*, and the Goofe was to be *au dernier gout*. To be brief, then, a part of the breaft fell to my fhare, which was fomething better than a hern or a fea-gull; but had a ftrong, oily, unpalatable flavour; of a blackifh colour, and fo very tender, that it gave me the opportunity of putting a bit into the orifice of my ftomach, which, by this time, began to be rapacious for want of fomething to devour. However, plenty of good Claret and

and agreeable converfation made up other deficiencies; and I took my leave in very good humour, though heartily praying never to be invited again to a dinner in *the higheft Tafte*, where I muft facrifice my own to conform to the caprice of fome pampered glutton, whofe *want of Tafte* has been able to gain credit in the world, and fet a fafhion.

As I am on the fubject of eating, I will finifh this with mentioning three other difhes which are common in this country; Cabbiclow, Barley-broth, and Friars-chicken. The firft is cod-fifh falted for a fhort time, and not dried in the manner of common falt-fifh, and boiled with parfley and horfe-radifh. They eat it with egg fauce, and it is extremely lufcious and palatable. Barley-broth is beef ftewed with a quantity of pearl barley and greens of different forts: and the other is. Chicken cut into fmall pieces, and boiled with parfley, cinnamon, and eggs, in ftrong beef foup. I know not what holy order may have had the reputation of difcovering this laft difh; but,

but, from the luxurioufnefs of it, it feems admirably adapted for the provifion of a convent.

I remain, with beft refpects,

 your ever devoted friend,

  and obliged, humble fervant,

LETTER

LETTER XX.

The Feudal System, and its Consequences.

To R. D. Esq;

Edinburgh, February 9, 1775.

SIR,

I Make no doubt but you will agree with me in thinking, that the Feudal System was the most unfriendly one that could have been devised for the happiness of mankind. Without dwelling upon the baneful influence which it had over the morals of the people, in making them ever ready at the call of their Chieftains, for acts of violence and oppression, it is sufficiently against it to say, that it was totally subversive of industry and improvements of every kind. In all the countries where the peasants are subject to this mode of government, they are fond of solitude, neglectful of themselves, and totally void of that active principle which leads men into public society, which animates them against every obstacle, and at length opens their way to riches. In all the northern parts, where a ſtate of villanage exiſts to this day, the introduction of trade and agriculture have in vain been attempted: for what argument can perſuade a man to be induſtrious, when he is liable every moment to be deprived of the rewards of it? or what care will he take to improve a poſſeſſion, the very tenure of which is precarious? Amongſt all the latter improvements that have been made in Germany, Denmark, and Ruſſia, this right has been given up, and the Empreſs, who has given an aſylum to all the fugitives from Poland, has encouraged the riſe of agriculture, by introducing the Engliſh ſyſtem of renting farms on leaſe.

Though this mode of government has long been aboliſhed in Scotland, the people feel the effects of it to this day. In many parts of the Highlands, they are yet totally ignorant of all the arts of agriculture: they never think of manuring the ground; they do not attempt trying the different graſſes on ſpots near their habitation, or of draining the wet parts, many of which are highly capable
of

of cultivation, as they are entirely sheltered by the hills which rise above them; or even of taking the trouble to pick up the loose stones which lie every where under their feet, to make a fence. They live poor, as their fathers did before them, and nothing seems hereditary but idleness. They place their sole dependence on grazing, since this mode of farming can be pursued with scarce any trouble to themselves, as their cattle range about for food, while they throw themselves on the grass, and sleep by them.

As this system of government effectually prevented the labours of the husbandman during its continuance, it likewise deprived him of all attachment to his native country. Wherever he cast his eyes, he saw no works of his hands, no fruits of his industry, no scenes of his own creation, to claim his attention: all was a barren solitude, from which he could never change but for the better. It is from this principle they have become a nation of wanderers by profession. That the lower class of people in the Highlands have no local attachments, the late numerous emigrations to America will sufficiently testify: and, probably, this is one of the least equivocal proofs that can be given of some great fault in the original plan of this kind of government, more than of any dislike to their present landlords, when a large body of people can by any means be induced to quit a country where they have been bred, and become adventurers: when they can be persuaded to forsake those known habitations, however poor, where they have passed their lives, and trust to the mercy of a country where they have no friends to receive them, and in which they have new settlements to form.

The inhabitants of the Lowlands have equally manifested that restless desire of travelling, which a want of employment at home naturally inspires. Go into what country you will, you always find Scotchmen. They penetrate into every climate: you meet with them in all the various departments of travellers, soldiers, merchants, adventurers, domestics. Consult the history of their own nation from the earliest period, and that of other nations, and you will find, that if any dangerous and difficult enterprize has been undertaken, any uncommon proofs given of patience or activity, any new countries visited and improved, that a Scotchman has borne some share in the performance. If the Scotch are to be found guilty of being national, it is not that they are attached to this mountain or to that district, but that they are partial to each other. It is not that they love the country, but their friends. You will, however, imagine, from what I have said, that I by no means join in this charge against them; on the contrary, I think it has no foundation. It has been the illiberal and disgraceful principle of these times, to hold the Scotch deserving of every reproach, and to load them with all the invectives, that either ill-manners or ill-will could suggest. They have been abused, not because they were really bad men, but Scotchmen, as if climate inferred infamy. And, if after all this, some Scotchman, as was very natural, not entirely callous to this treatment of his countrymen, arose to justify them; the cry immediately was, he was national. Lord Bute was supposed to be the fountain of all this evil: he probably thought it was necessary to take some notice of his friends in their adversity. There was, however, this to be said of it, that as the name of Scotchman was no absolute recommendation, he must have had some merit of his own; whereas an Englishman has often been taken notice of, merely for being such.

But what merits observation amongst this people most is, that tho' they are lazy and improvident at home, though they discover a total dislike and contempt of labour in their own country, the very same men become the most industrious and frugal abroad, and evince a capacity and an invention worthy the imitation of all nations. It is in their own climate alone that their abilities seem to lie dormant; they wait for other suns to call them forth into life, and to give animation to their sleeping faculties. The workmen of this country are esteemed throughout Europe for their peculiar sobriety and attention: and the military profession all allow, that no soldiers whatever are more courageous;

rageous, or more patient of fatigue in war: none that are more obedient in peace, or that make a better appearance with the small pittance which the pay of a common soldier allows him.

The most ingenious artists now in London are Scotchmen, and are as remarkable for the diligence with which they pursue their trade, as they are for the many admirable improvements they have made in its various branches. All who have seen Mr. Brodie's manufactories in cast iron, and Mr. Tassie's compositions in imitation of the *antique*, will join in the truth of this observation: and what is equally to their credit, you see no assumed airs of importance, no consciousness of their own abilities; but a civility, and an attention in every thing. The most ingenious artificer now in Paris is a Scotchman. He begged his bread from the northernmost part of the Highlands up to London, where, after several progressive steps of wretchedness and misery, he was admitted to sweep the shop of a Jeweller. By a long course of attentive observation, he obtained some little insight

insight into the rudiments of the business; and having always laid up very carefully what his civility to the customers of the shop got him, he at last scraped together a few pounds. With this he travelled to Paris, where he was taken by a Jeweller of some eminence. His master, who observed his honesty and abilities, furnished him with five hundred crowns, when his time of apprenticeship expired; and from this small sum, by a gradual increase of business, which his taste in designs, and his elegance in working, has procured him, he is become one of the first tradesmen in Paris.

Had this man met with encouragement at home, it is more than probable, that he never would have left his native country: and the same abilities, which made him distinguished in this business, would have made equally so in one more useful to society.

Thus destructive has been the influence of a System of Government, which once kept the greatest part of Europe in a subjection as disgraceful to the natural
freedom

freedom of society, as it was unfavourable to the industry of individuals. These ingenious natives, who could not expect any advantages at home, were obliged to seek those rewards abroad, which their own country denied to them: and, probably, a century ago, Scotland was the only kingdom in Europe, which had not been benefited by the labours of Scotchmen.

In my next letter, I will send you an account of what improvements have been lately made in this country, and which, though at present in their infancy, are an earnest of their future excellence.

I have the honour to be, &c.

LETTER

LETTER XXI.

The different Manufactures of Scotland.

To R. D. Esq.

Edinburgh, February 18, 1775.

SIR,

WITHIN these few years Scotland has worn a very different appearance from what it formerly did; and though, as yet, it cannot vie with the later and more luxurious improvements of some nations, it now has the ample means of furnishing employment for the greatest part of its own inhabitants. The mechanic Arts, Trade, Agriculture, Manufactories, are no longer the offspring of a day, or scarce conscious of their existence, but wear the promising marks of future vigour and stability.

The manufactories, now established in many parts of this country, are all in a very flourishing condition: that for the making tapes, threads, garters, &c. at Glasgow, has not only enriched its owners, but been the means of

breaking

breaking up most of the same sort in England. The cheapness of labour here has enabled the proprietors to undersell the English above *5 per cent.* and as they equal the English tapes in colour and quality, all the London merchants almost now buy from hence. But besides this branch of wholesale trade, there is a species of retail which, in the aggregate, is full as profitable, or more so; and which, though it may not be considered in the great scale of business, is still the best branch of it: these are all the persons who, under the denomination of Pedlars, travel through different countries, and, being most of them Scotchmen, dispose of these articles to the lower classes of people, at a great profit to themselves, as well as ultimately enriching their own country.

The manufactory of Stockings in the country about Aberdeen is now very great, and finds employment for many thousands, who are as frugal as they are industrious; for while they are furnishing many parts of Europe with stockings, they themselves go without them. Almost every part of every family is engaged in this branch of business,

from

from the master of the whole to the smallest children in it.

The Linen trade, which seems the favourite one in Scotland, has had great additions and improvements lately made to it, and is still increasing: had the late design here been carried into act of Parliament, this business would have been put on the most respectable footing, and would have extended its sale much beyond the present limits. A large hall, like those in Leeds, and some other places in England, has been erected in this town for the reception of linen, and to accommodate the purchasers. The late Lord Milton interested himself much in the success of this trade, and, by many judicious regulations, has contributed much to its present state. But the Irish, who excell the Scotch in all the finer linens, must always keep them down: and it is from this superiority in particular, that the Scotch ought to be convinced, that the linen manufactory should not be the only object of their attention. At best it can have but a divided sale in England, and in all probability the worst share. The Scotch, however, excell the Irish in that species of linen which

is

is calculated for the table: the ſtrength and the beauty of the interwoven patterns in this article, exceed any thing the Iriſh have produced. Formerly the Scotch uſed to ſend ſome of their fineſt linens to be bleached at Haerlem in Holland; but they found it did not anſwer the expence of it; as the freight, and other articles, made it dearer by ten pence a yard: they now bleach it entirely amongſt themſelves; and as they have good water and good grounds, I ſee no reaſon for ſending it from home.

But their chief manufactory, and that on which, in my opinion, the Scotch ought to rely, is their Carpets: many other countries will rival, if not exceed them, in their other branches; but in this they are without a competitor. In many articles their ſucceſs hitherto has been owing to the cheapneſs of their labour: in this its excellence alone has been its beſt recommendation. The ſale which theſe Carpets meet with in England is aſtoniſhing: you find them in every houſe, from the higheſt to the loweſt, as they are calculated to ſuit that claſs of people who wiſh for the conveniencies of life, but who

cannot

cannot afford the extravagant prices of Wilton, Axminster, and other more expensive manufactories. They have been, in a great measure, the means of rendering the houses here so comfortable, and are the best securities against stone buildings, stone stair-cases, and a cold climate. As yet their artists have not arrived at much elegance in the design or brilliancy of colour: but these improvements follow of course; the embellishments of art and luxury always succeed to convenience. In some pieces that I have seen, which have been made by particular orders, great taste has been shewn: a proof that an idea, as yet, probably, in its infancy, has been started of improvements in this article. When those improvements take place, and the period will not be far distant, this manufactory may be as much distinguished for its elegance, as it is now for its goodness.

An attempt has been made to introduce a manufactory of Cambrick, adjoining to Edinburgh; but without much success: It is not so fine, by many degrees, as the French; and, I am informed, not near so durable. It likewise loses its colour in washing. A few people who travelled here from Picardy, brought this along with them; but, unhappily, though they brought the art of making it, they could not bring the materials. These people, however, deserve encouragement: the man who hazards his fortune, and probably his life, by carrying over an art from his own country into another, should it even fail of success, is still deserving of reward from the country he intended to benefit.

It is from these means that exclusive trades can never be long carried on. What has been found to be beneficial in one country, will always be the object of desire in another; and there are always men to be met with, who, from pecuniary advantages, may be drawn over to introduce it. Inflict personal or other punishments as you will, the artificer who has not sufficient employment at home, will always go where he can live best, and act the master. It is from this general dispersion of trade and manufactories in every country, that immense wealth is no longer to be expected by any one in prejudice of all the rest. The Dutch, who carried this point higher than any other nation, have already seen the best days of their commerce, and feel their decline. The manufactories of Delft, which once supplied all Europe, do not at present supply even themselves: they bring over from England the Queen's Ware, the improvement of their own idea. Some other country may put an end to ours in its turn. What right have we then to complain of the instability of one man's fortune, when the great manufactures of a nation, when the trade of a whole country, are thus subject to vicissitudes? There is this consolation left us, that the steps are slowly taken, and that many generations must pass away in the progress of each. Those people, however, are the most happy, who live in that brightest period of every government, when arts and sciences, when luxury and opulence, when improvements of every kind, are at their height; who partake of these blessings, and die before their decline.

I have the honour to be, &c.

LETTER

LETTER XXII.

The Scotch Bookfellers; their Publications, &c.

To R. D. Efq;

Edinburgh, February 23, 1775.

SIR,

THE moſt profitable trade now in Edinburgh appears to be that of a Bookſeller. Of all the other advantageous branches this place has only received a part in conjunction with many other towns in Scotland; but they have appropriated this buſineſs at preſent entirely to themſelves. If I am well informed, many thouſand volumes are annually printed in this place, and ſold in London or elſewhere. The cheapneſs of labour here, when compared with London, induces many Scotch Bookſellers who reſide there, to have their books printed at Edinburgh, and then ſent to them; which they find much better than printing at their own ſhops: and for this purpoſe, many of them have partners in this place.

Some years ago the Printing-office at Glasgow was a formidable rival to that at Edinburgh; and had the two celebrated Printers there purſued their buſineſs, they might have carried away the whole trade of Scotland to themſelves. [But, alas! "Men are but men," as Triſtram Shandy obſerves, " and the beſt " have their weakneſſes." An unfortunate deſire ſeized theſe two gentlemen of inſtituting an academy of painting, and of buying a collection of pictures; forgetting that the place where this academy was to be inſtituted was amongſt a ſociety of tradeſmen, who would throw away no money on ſuch ſubjects. With this idea they bought paintings which nobody elſe will buy again, and which now lie upon their hands in high preſervation. During the rage of this fancy, they forgot their former buſineſs, and neglected an art which, from their editions of Homer and Milton, might have made them immortal, to run after paltry copies of good paintings, which they had been informed were originals.

When I viſited theſe gentlemen I had heard of their Printing, but never of their Academy. It was in vain that I aſked for books; I had always

always a picture thrust into my hand; and like Boniface, though they had nothing in print worth notice, they said they could shew me a delicate engraving. You may well imagine that this ambition has prevented their former success: for though Poetry and Painting may be sister arts, I never heard that Painting and Printing were of the same family; if they are, their interests have been very opposite.

Banished from Glasgow this trade has settled at Edinburgh, and by the ingenuity and application of those who are engaged in it, has been brought to great perfection. I mean that perfection which includes every requisite in a book for the smallest price possible.

A bookseller in this city, who is not only a polite man, but a man of letters, is now printing a complete set of the English Classics in duodecimo; which, with the addition of a very handsome binding, amount only to eighteen pence a volume. It is such productions as these that do honour to a country; and I confess I feel a pleasure in reflecting that this has been the work of a Scotch Bookseller, as it seems some sort of compensation for the blow which was given by their means to literature in general.

In regard to this decifion, fo much has already been faid upon it, as well as written; fo many judicious arguments advanced on both fides, during the long trial it gave rife to, that no new light could be thrown upon the fubject. But I cannot help declaring, that I think it was the moft unfortunate decifion ever pronounced by a court of judicature. You will eafily believe that I am not led away by any partiality to this or that Bookfeller: I think both the Scotch and the Englifh ones acted as any other people would have acted, who had very important interefts at ftake. But without confidering the right which any act of Parliament has to deprive a man of his own private property, whatever that property may be, I am forry, for the fake of literature, that fuch a decifion was ever given; and I cannot but feel for the loffes which a number of learned and ingenious men muft feel, whofe works have frequently been their only fupport.

The rewards of literary merit have always been, comparatively, too fmall. A man or
abilities,

abilities, for instance, in the profession of Law or Physic, who benefits only individuals, and whose abilities, generally speaking, are employed as much to the prejudice as the advantage of mankind, shall receive many thousands a year: while another man, whose education has been equally expensive to him, whose labours are not confined to one age or country, whose works must have an useful tendency, or the public would discourage them, such a man shall lead a life devoted to study and confinement, while the only recompence he receives for all his toils shall be a bare subsistence. There never was an instance of a man acquiring a fortune by the sale of his writings: there are a thousand, in which the most ingenious men have languished during their whole lives in poverty and obscurity. We have had too many unfortunate instances in our own country, to make it necessary to quote the examples of poor Camoens or Bentivoglio; though the fate of this latter is truly singular:—The Comedies which he wrote, and which are an honour to the Italian language, are a sufficient proof of his abilities. He dissipated, as his story tells us, us, a large fortune in various acts of charity; and becoming himself an object of compassion in his old age, he was refused admittance into an hospital which he had erected for the benefit of others. Modern times can shew equal ingenuity on the one hand, and equal ingratitude on the other. The late Mr. Smollet, whose abilities every one is acquainted with, wrote for a number of years without procuring to himself any thing more than a livelihood: And Dr. Goldsmith, whose poverty obliged him to write so much and so variously, that, had he lived many years longer, in all probability his imagination and his subsistence would have failed together, found that all his talents could barely secure him from indigence: his whole life was a tissue of distress and genius, of merit and suffering.

It is from these motives that I wish for every encouragement to be given to Authors; and there was no other way of doing it effectually than by affixing every possible degree of value to their works. Booksellers cannot be blamed for not giving the same price for a lease of fourteen years, that they would for the perpetuity:

petuity: but what is peculiarily hard is, that this act falls the heaviest on the most ingenious men. Those who write for the day are also forgotten with the day: their labours can expect no longer date. But there are men of real genius, many of which this country can boast, whose works will survive that period, yet become circumscribed by these limits, and lose half their value.

From this decision the Scotch Booksellers may date the æra of their success in this trade: for they will always flourish so long as the comparative cheapness of their workmen enables them to undersell the London Bookseller with profit to themselves. Hitherto they have printed those authors only whose right was expired to the proprietors; as all the late works of their own writers have been bought and printed in London; and, indeed, will always be so, while the best prices are given them.

But a trade which does not depend entirely on its own merit, but on the small expence at which its articles are procured, can only succeed so long as those articles continue cheap. Holland, which once supplied

plied the greatest part of Europe, failed in that branch as soon as the paper became cheaper in France than in their own country.

Though the Scotch are certainly a very ingenious people, and in general good writers, you see very few publications make their appearance. You are pestered with none of those weekly, daily, and almost hourly pamphlets, which every where meet one's eye in London, under the names of Nuptial Elegies, Sentimental Scruples, Juvenile Poems, Amorous Epistles, and a thousand others of the same ingenious and tender natures. Such delicate productions would expire in this cold climate, as they owe their birth to idle hours and mild skies.

The only publications which appear constantly are the Newspapers, a Magazine, and a Review, which are executed nearly in the same style as those in London.

Not long ago, a little pamphlet made its appearance, complaining of some abuses committed in the management, or rather mismanagement of an hospital here, and dedicated to the most impudent man alive.

You

You will confess that this title was rather disputable. One gentleman, however, by being very angry, shewed he had some right to the dedication, from thus openly asserting his claim to it. How happy would it be for society, if some one could always be found to avow his right to all those defamatory invectives, those allegories of abuse, which are frequently lavished on individuals by anonymous writers, and which terrify a thousand innocent people, but leave the guilty unknown.

I have the honour to be, &c.

LETTER

LETTER XXIII.

Some Observations on the Kirk, and Devotion of the People, English Chapel, &c.

To T. M. Esq.

Edinburgh, March 3, 1775.

DEAR SIR,

I Have been now resident in this city so considerable a time, that I begin to look on myself, and indeed wish to be thought by the inhabitants of it, almost a native of the country. In all respects I have endeavoured to accommodate myself to their manners and customs, as, in my opinion, every stranger ought to do in a foreign climate; and am become so habituated to them, that I consider them as my own.

It gives me much concern to inform you, there are already in this place more clergymen of the Church of England, than are necessary to perform the duty required; that it will be to no purpose for your friend to come to settle here in expectation of employment

ployment in his function. There are at present six or seven, and some without any duty, occasioned by a schism amongst them, and the governors of the New Chapel. But the discarded gentlemen say, the governors have no right to turn them out, *et adhuc sub judice lis est*. I am the more sorry to send you this unfavourable account, since I am sure your friend would be no unacceptable addition to them, as there is not one who can be called a good reader, or an orator in the pulpit; so far from it, that I never attended to more insignificant, unprofitable discourses in any church. Even the Presbyterians, who preach without book, and consequently ought to have every allowance made them, excel them in such a manner, that I am astonished any reasonable man, whatever may be the mode of worship in his own country, should think it worth his time to listen to them.

The Ministers of the Church of Scotland assume a virtue, if they have it not; and I must say for them, (though it is incredible what nonsense I have sometimes heard from their pulpits) that they command attention,
even

even when you are shocked at the absurdity of their language: whereas those of the English Chapel, drone out their common-place precepts of morality with so much coldness and indifference, that it is with difficulty you can yawn out a sermon. Indeed, this real or pretended godliness is not confined to the Ministers of the Church of Scotland; but is universal, especially on a Sabbath. During the time of Kirk, you scarcely see any body in the streets, or loitering away the time of prayer in wantonness and excess: though, at other times, and even then in private, there is no crime they would scruple to commit. To be seen in the street after the summons of the bell, or to read any book on a Sunday which has no relation to religion, seems wicked and abominable to the most abandoned. You must acknowledge, it redounds greatly to the credit of Presbyterianism, that the mask of religion should bear so strong a resemblance to the reality; for, in general, good consequences must arise from it. "I never can imagine but that the person, who lays so much stress upon the apparent and outward part of his duty, must have a sufficient

sufficient inward sense of it, as would frequently lead him to the discharge and observance of those offices which can only arise from the heart, and which cannot be supposed to spring from a desire of applause or profit." But you may object, that this parade of goodness is greatly instrumental to hypocrisy and deceit. Perhaps it may in some measure: but surely the evil, which may arise from that, is abundantly counter-balanced by the advantages derived from it to society, if it is only in keeping the conscience awake, that silent monitor of what is good and right. Whereas, in London, what other difference do the common people make in Sunday, except in the excess of idleness and riot? But far be it from me to say, that the Scotch nation have more real religion than the English: I only affirm, let their principles be what they may, that there is a greater appearance of regard to public worship, and more respect paid to the Sabbath. I must not forget to mention the extraordinary neatness and simplicity of dress, which distinguish them at this time of public prayer. The poorest cottager,

cottager, with his best face, puts on his best apparel, as it were, to present himself at the throne of mercy, a pure and unpolluted sacrifice. The Kirks also, in general, are plain, unadorned, and such large edifices, that they contain the most numerous congregations. I am told, the Trone Church would hold, with ease, at least fifteen hundred persons.

With respect to their discourses from the pulpit, which are delivered as it were by inspiration, was I to speak in dispraise of them, you might think, perhaps, I was too much bigotted in favour of the Church of England, to give an impartial account; I shall only inform you, therefore, that their sermons are longer and not so correct as those of our clergymen; but better calculated for the generality of congregations; being addressed more to the passions, and never on any abstract topics of divinity, which are unintelligible to the common people. Indeed this may be one reason why the common people so universally frequent the Kirk; for, if they gain no instruction, they are sure to be entertained, and have

have their underftandings flattered. It is really a curious fight to behold, at the conclufion of the meeting, the inundation of people that flow from the Kirks, on account of their being fo crowded. I have feen the High Street in Edinburgh, which is no inconfiderable one, from having the appearance of a deferted place, fo " thronged," as they call it, with people in ten minutes, that it was nearly impoffible to pafs by.

It would be needlefs for me to fay any thing concerning the tenets of the Prefbyterians, or their mode of worfhip to you, who muft be fo much better acquainted with them: I have, therefore, taken the liberty, as I know you are a ftranger to Scotland, to mention thofe circumftances only, which may not have come within your hearing, as they relate, perhaps, folely to the Prefbyterians in this country.

The New Englifh Chapel is a neat, elegant building, but hardly large enough for the Members of the Church of England, who are conftant inhabitants of this City. The architect has been fo unfortunate in his pofition of the pulpit, that, in particular places, the voice of the preacher is totally confounded by the echo. An excellent organ attracts by its novelty, as nothing of that kind is admitted in the Kirks.

I am your obliged friend, &c.

LETTER XXIV.

On the Dress of the better Sort of the Inhabitants of Edinburgh.

To Miss Sophia D———

Edinburgh, March 6, 1775.

MY DEAR MADAM,

I Received your kind letter; am sensible of the obligation I owe you for it, and take this first opportunity of discharging my debt as well as I am able; though I am sorry to say, I must act after the manner of all other bankrupts, and pay you but a part of the whole.

The entertainment which you afforded me by your descriptions, and your drawing of the present mode of dressing the hair, I was not so much a miser as to keep to myself. It gives me much surprise to find the extravagance of the ladies head-dress still increases; as I imagined it had been before elevated to a degree, that must have made it inconvenient and troublesome.

Because,

Becaufe, for inftance, the Dutchefs of D— has a head capable of bearing its weight, and features, complexion, and figure, which become a towering plume of party-coloured feathers, I dare fay there will not be a face ever fo ill-favoured, a fkin of the coarfeft grain, or a diftorted fhape in the Pantheon for the remainder of the winter, without this aërial ornament. The Englifh women are not Amazonian enough in general to make them look proportionate or graceful; for they certainly have a mafculine appearance, and give you the idea of a helmet. A fhort woman in this difguife muft put you in mind of the armed head that makes fo formidable a figure among the ghofts in Macbeth. But I know you will elude all I can urge, by faying it is the Fafhion, which muft be conformed to, and which makes every thing agreeable. I grant it in fome meafure. Pleafure is what we all fo ftedfaftly purfue, that there needs only Fafhion to give any thing that name; and the defire of imitation will make it followed, till the force of cuftom has rendered it agreeable. But ftill I have no notion of an univerfal fafhion. I would
have

have every one suit their height, colour, and dimensions, and then I should have no objection to feathers, or to see a gigantic woman nodding with the tail of an ostrich, whilst the beautiful concisenefs of Miss S——'s person would confine itself to the modest plumage of the turtle-dove. Indeed, I am so far from looking with perfect dislike on this mode of wearing feathers, that I think it might be made of great utility to our sex, if the ladies would but choose the feathers of such birds as in some measure were emblematical of their dispositions or rank. Suppose her Majesty, for instance, were to appear at court with the feathers of the princely eagle, whilst my lady Mayoress assumed the pompous insignificance of the turkey-cock— Coquets might be furnished from the species of parrots—the goose might fit out the old maid; the peacock vindicate the dowager; whilst the wanton sparkling widow might mourn under the umbrage of the raven or the magpye. But you ask me, if this fashion has extended its flight this way? I am happy to tell you, it has not; though I must think it would be more applicable to the

beauty

beauty of this country, than to that of ours.

The women here do not so readily adopt any trifling fashion from London. They conform themselves much more to the manners and taste of Paris, with which they have as constant a communication as with England. The Ladies in Edinburgh dress, in general, with more elegance, and in a way better accommodated to their persons, size, and shape, than most of the European nations; whilst they are peculiarly attentive to the nature of their climate and seasons, as well as to their age, after the manner of the French. You never see the mortifying spectacle of an old woman displayed in all the shew and vanity of a boarding-school Miss; or the widowed wife of nineteen assuming the air and dress of an ancient married matron, in order to adapt herself to the age of a decrepid and peevish husband—In a morning also their dress is equally becoming; their dishabille is never negligent and loose, but neat and plain, with a degree of smartness and elegance; and a genius for dress even then discovers itself, just as you may see the masterly

strokes

strokes of a poet, in two or three unpremeditated *extempore* verses. But I wish I could say as much for the men: they neither take so much care of their persons or appearance; nor have they half the taste in their dress that the Ladies have, who choose the most becoming fashions from London and Paris, and form one of their own, more graceful, perhaps, than either. But the Gentlemen neither know how, nor are studious of setting off their figure to advantage. In the politest assemblies in this City, you rarely see a Gentleman well-dressed: In those that think themselves the best, there is always some deficiency; whilst you will not find one Lady without every assistance of ornament and art; and an ill-dressed Lady is as great a novelty as an ill-bred one.

But however they may be indebted to external shew, or whatever they may have borrowed from the French, they derive none of their beauty from paint, nor have they had folly enough to imitate that nation in this absurd fashion. Indeed, neither their colour nor complexion stand in need of it; for I know not where they will find their equals in either.

ther. But if that was a reason, we should not see so many charming faces concealed by it in London, where it often happens that, under this disguise, a more beautiful countenance is hid, than that which is presented to the public. For my own part, I have such a detestation of this species of painting, that I would rather behold the most ugly, mis-shapen face as God made it, than rendered comely and inanimate by this plastering of art. One may as well salute a picture or a statue. None but a Pygmalion could fall in love with them. Besides, this fashion has not even that to recommend it, which is common to all others, how absurd soever, *viz.* of being of advantage to some trade or commerce. If all the Ladies in a city were to paint, one Perfume-shop might supply them all, and have no great business: whereas the difference of shape, figure, and colour of cloaths, furnish many manufactures with employ, and the industrious artificer with an honest livelihood. In this case the constant change of fashions is of much utility to a country: though I think there is nothing that is a greater proof of the natural

instability

inſtability of our minds and opinions, or that ſhews in a clearer light the caprice and fickleneſs of human nature. One could hardly imagine a rational creature ſhould think it worth while to concern himſelf with ſuch trifles; or that a Being, whoſe life is but a ſpan, ſhould ſpend the few moments allotted him, in altering the dimenſions of his habit, or changing, perhaps, only the form of his hat: but ſuch is our conſtitution;—We fluctuate between various inclinations—Every day a new whim: our humour keeps motion with the time, and we follow the inclination of our fancy according as we are wafted by the breath of occaſion. But I already hear you ſay, " And what art thou, poor mora-" lizer?" No ſolitary fly, I aſſure you. I am here in the midſt of entertainment, noiſe, and company; and would not change my ſituation, unleſs for the happineſs of a converſation with you, for the profit of half the land that is between us.

After all this, you will find yourſelf highly miſtaken in your opinion of this nation and its manners: and I cannot but tell you, you are not more ſo in any particular, than in
your

your notions concerning their drefs. You think alfo their hair is inclinable to red. The womens hair is either a dark brown, or perfectly red, which I efteem a very beautiful colour, and is that which in ancient times was fo admired, received the appellation of golden, and was given by way of diftinction to a Pallas or a Juno. I am forry to fay the Ladies here often conceal it by powder, having the fame idea of it that you have, and making no difference between it, and that fandy-coloured red, which, of all hair, is the moft difagreeable and unbecoming. In moft refpects they drefs their hair with great elegance and propriety, in no extremes, neither too elevated nor too depreffed, but in that juft-proportioned medium, which is always the refult of tafte and judgment. As to hoops, they feldom ufe them, and add very little to their height by the heels of their shoes. The Gentlemen, after the cuftom of the French, wear their hair in bags, efpecially the Advocates and Profeffors of the College, who commonly drefs in black. With refpect to cloaths, as I faid before, I cannot speak in great praife of them; and they

have

have the worst taylors, perhaps, in the world.

And now, my dear Sophia, I must wish you farewell. Be assured, I can find no greater pleasure than in receiving your letters, with which I hope you will be so kind as to indulge me whenever you have an idle hour; as I am, with the truest sincerity and friendship,

your ever affectionate,

and obliged humble servant.

LETTER XXV.

On the College of Edinburgh, &c.

To Dr. M. at Oxford.

Edinburgh, March 13, 1775.

I Received your obliging and polite letter from the Univerſity; and am very happy to find, that our friend Mr. D—— has had the ſucceſs which I am ſenſible he merited, both as a ſcholar and a gentleman. Happy would the world be if every man, who had as much learning, was equally fortunate; and I think I may ſay, happy would it be for the Univerſity of Oxford, if the inſtruction of the riſing generation was ever committed to the care of thoſe, who are as worthy of ſetting them

them an example of civility and good manners, as of morality and virtue. I muſt own that, in this reſpect, the Profeſſors of the College of Edinburgh ſhine conſpicuous: and though all of them are men of letters, and ſkilled in the ſciences they profeſs, they are not leſs acquainted with the world, and with polite behaviour, than with polite literature.

The College is a very ancient and irregular building, conſiſting of three courts on different planes, which are ſmall, and contain rooms for the Profeſſors to read their lectures. I do not find any of the Profeſſors inhabit the College, except the Principal, who lives in a houſe which ſtands where formerly was ſituated the houſe of the Provoſt of the Kirk of Field, blown up by gunpowder A. D. 1567, to conceal the murder of Henry Huſband, to Queen Mary.

As being the foundation of the Citizens, the College is in the patronage of the Magiſtrates and Town Council of Edinburgh; who,

who, as Curators, have the management of its revenues. Oliver Cromwel, A. D. 1658, gave towards its support an Annuity of two hundred pounds sterling; and the whole annual expences of it amount to 2000 l. The poor Students, who resemble the Scholars in our Universities, are fifty-one in number; they have different sums allowed them, and five of them have ten pounds a year: they wear no gowns, and have no marks of distinction, as at Glasgow and St. Andrews.

The Library is well furnished with books in variety of languages and sciences. There is a picture in it of Lord Napier of Marcheston, the celebrated inventor of the logarithms; and a very curious copy of a double-faced letter, written by Cardinal Richelieu to the Embassador of France at Rome, concerning a Benedictine Monk, which implies either the best or the most villainous character.

In this, as in all the other Colleges of Scotland, till of late, were only taught Divinity,

vinity, School-philosophy, Mathematics, and Languages: but in the last reigns, the number of Professors was so augmented, that nothing is wanting to form a complete academical education; since all the liberal arts are taught as in the other celebrated universities in Europe. Divinity, Church History, Civil Law, the Law of Nature and Nations, and Scotch Law, Anatomy, Theory of Physic, Practice of Physic, Chymistry, Botany, Mathematics, Universal History, Natural Philosophy, Logic, Metaphysics, and Ethics, Greek, Latin, and Hebrew languages, have each their respective Professor; and as the sciences of Divinity and Mathematics, and the Greek tongue have two Professors, the number of the whole amounts to twenty-one, and the sciences taught by them eighteen. Their salaries are different; the largest is that of the Professor of the Law of Nature and Nations, being one hundred and fifty pounds, and the lowest is thirty-three pounds sterling: but the number of students that frequent the College amply re-
compense

compense them for the trouble and expence of lectures.

As the University of Edinburgh is celebrated throughout Europe for its instruction in particular branches of philosophy and literature, the number of young persons that crowd here from different countries is prodigious, and the profit arising from them is sensibly perceived through all Scotland, as they contribute to the support of many thousands of its inhabitants, in supplying either their necessities or luxury by their manufactures and industry. They are under no restraint from the College, but have lodgings in the City. In general they are very extravagant, especially those from Ireland, who too often forsake the calm, retired paths of learning and science, to revel in the public scenes of dissipation and debauchery. But the students who are natives of this country, present a different picture. The miserable holes which some of them inhabit, their abstemiousness and parsimony,. their constant attendance to study, their indefatigable industry, even border on romance. They
seem

seem to look on learning as a diversion, and when once they have roused her from her abstruse and concealed haunts, never quit her footsteps, till they have pursued her to the covert. But, in general, they apply themselves to too many of the Professors, to pay a proper attention to each; and their excessive earnestness to obtain an universal knowledge, hinders them from gaining that proficiency in any one science, which ought to be the object of great minds. I take this to be one reason of that mediocrity of learning, which Dr. Johnson speaks of in his Tour, and which is to be found in every part of Scotland. For, as the lectures of the Professors are open to every one, and the expence of attending them very trifling, it is in the power of almost every tradesman to furnish his son with that instruction which is most adapted to his taste or capacity, and is the reason why the middle degree of people are not in such a state of ignorance as in England and in other countries. On the contrary, the easy access to the lectures is an inducement to those whose fortune and circumstances can support the expence, to attend

attend so many, that the knowledge which they acquire must be imperfect and superficial.

The College of Edinburgh does not differ more from the Universities of England in any respect than in this; that every age and every rank have a liberty of choosing such lectures as are most suited to their inclination, pleasures, or pursuits in life; whereas, at Oxford and Cambridge, a young man is no sooner inlisted under the banners of *alma mater*, but he is compelled to listen to sciences for which he has no taste, neglects those studies to which his genius points, and by the time he arrives at that age when serious thoughts and calm reflection should disclose the pleasures of reason and philosophy, he is obliged to behold them with contempt and disdain, because he finds them the objects of striplings and schoolboys.

I remain yours sincerely.

LETTER

LETTER XXVI.

On the Lectures of the College; Mode of reading them; and Observations on some of the Professors of the College.

To the Reverend Dr. M——, at Oxford.

Edinburgh, March 15, 1775.

DEAR SIR,

AS I am not one of those persons who affect to stand on punctilio at any time; it would be unpardonable in me to wait the arrival of an answer to my last letter: when I am sufficiently conscious your time is never employed to so little purpose as in writing to me; and my own never so well, as in testifying my gratitude for the innumerable obligations I lie under to your friendship.

Since my last, I may almost say I am again commenced Academician: I have attended some of the Professors Lectures, and find in them so much entertainment, that I propose, for the future, spending some hours with them every day. But I cannot say their company are the most agreeable companions; the Scotch students not being so remarkable for their cleanliness and politeness as for their poverty, famine, and science.

I believe, I before omitted giving you any information concerning the mode of reading lectures: I must just tell you, therefore, that each Professor has his room or theatre; which is surrounded by benches, that have desks before them for the students to write and take notes; and the Professor stands, or is seated, in the middle, as is best adapted to the purport of his lecture. Most of the Professors wear gowns like those of our Universities; and their lecture, in general, lasts about three quarters of an hour.

As the College of Edinburgh has for many years been celebrated throughout Europe for its instruction in Physic, and the sciences which belong to it; you cannot but imagine that the greatest care is taken in the appointment of persons to the chair of those professorships which relate to this branch of knowledge;

knowledge; and indeed the electors gain great credit in the choice of all, there not being one who is not remarkable for his learning and abilities. The theory of Physic, Chemistry, and Anatomy, have Dr. Cullen, Dr. Black, and Dr. Munro: who are not more conspicuous for their skill in their profession, than for their knowledge of Philosophy and Mankind. But as the merit of these learned men must be as well known to you as to the rest of the world, who are at all acquainted with the sphere of literature; it would be needless for me to add my poor pittance of praise to characters which bear the stamp of general approbation. I shall only speak of them, therefore, as persons appointed to convey to the minds of youth that part of science which they profess, and of their manner of reading their lectures. In this last particular, I wish I could say as much in commendation of Dr. Cullen, as of many others: a dryness and insipidity in his delivery, with a want of energy in his manner, too often renders his lectures, which have every other merit, dull and uninterefting: but at the fame time it muft be acknowledged that his wonderful penetration and fagacity, his clearnefs and perfpicuity, his profound knowledge of the myfteries of his profeffion, make him the moft qualified to inftruct, and amply recompence any other deficiency.

The Profeffor of Chemiftry is too diffident of the juftnefs of his expreffion ever to appear an Orator: he is fo concife in his fentences, and at the fame time abounds in fuch a profufion of ideas, that it is with the greateft difficulty he can find words fatisfactory to himfelf: which might make many people imagine that he is ignorant of language. Indeed, fometimes he is at fuch a lofs to explain his meaning, that he is obliged to make a long paufe in his lecture; but when once his expreffion breaks forth, its propriety and ftrength more than reward your expectation: and no Chemift was ever more fuccefsful in his experiments than Dr. Black.

The Profeffor of Anatomy is the moft frequented of any of the Profeffors; as it is
neceffary

necessary for all the votaries of Esculapius to have a competent knowledge of this, as the foundation and ground-work of the other parts of Physic. Dr. Monro has all the advantages of a great Orator, full of strength and force in his expression, round and manly in his periods, emphatical and bold in his manner of delivery: he particularly avoids that familiarity, which too many of the Professors are apt to fall into in their lectures, and which seems to degrade their dignity by giving them the air of common conversation: and from this reason he appears to many to excel more in the physiological than in any other part of Anatomy; for the proper explanation of which an inferior manner might be better accommodated.

But before I quit this subject, I must not forget the Professor of Rhetoric; who, of all others, though perhaps not the most attended, claims the regard and observation of the polite scholar. The harmony of his diction, the elegance and sagacity of his criticisms, the proper modulation of his voice, the spirit and fire of his imagination, all confpire to make him that Orator which he wifhes to make his pupils. I need fay nothing further in commendation of Dr. Blair, than that all his lectures are compofed in the fame graceful ftyle, the fame fweetnefs of language, the fame vivacity of thought and nervous manlinefs, which is to be found in his " Effay on " the Poems of Ofcian," and which does not do him more credit as a fcholar, than as a man.

I have mentioned thefe Profeffors to you, as in general they are more known in the learned world than many of the others; but indeed moft of them are equally great and meritorious in their refpective offices: and I really believe, there is no part of the world where fo general an education can be obtained as in Edinburgh. I muft fay (and I flatter myfelf you will pardon my impartiality) it is my opinion, were our Univerfities on this plan as to inftruction, and, inftead of that diftinction of Tutors in different Colleges, a fet of the moft eminent Scholars were appointed to read lectures indifcriminately to the whole, it would

would be a confiderable ftep towards the advancement of learning and literature.

The College of Edinburgh confers degrees as the Univerfities of England and Scotland do: but no degree under a Doctor is of any eftimation; which may be had as foon as the neceffary inftruction can be acquired, to pafs the proper examination.

Believe me yours fincerely.

LETTER XXVII.

On Edinburgh as a Place of polite Education; with some Observations on their Trade, and Abilities for it.

To the Reverend Dr. M——, at Oxford.

Edinburgh, March 25, 1775.

DEAR SIR,

IN a former letter to you I considered Edinburgh as a seat of Learning, and peculiar for its instruction in the science of Physic: but I can assure you, that the Graces also deign to visit this northern climate; and by their frequent abode here, I should imagine, do not find it too cold for their constitution.

There are few places where a polite education can be better acquired than in this City; and where the knowledge requisite to form a Gentleman, and a Man of the World, can be sooner obtained. It is one of the greatest

faults

faults in our Universities, that so much attention and importance should be given to studies, which, perhaps, are of little use to a man in life, when either his fortune or dignity calls on him to exert his knowledge for the happiness of his fellow-countrymen: and, on the contrary, that those qualifications which make a man an amiable Friend, and an agreeable Companion, should be held in contempt, or perfectly neglected. But here it is quite otherwise. Each attends that system of Lectures which suit either his genius or intended pursuits, without restraint or compulsion. No particular study or science is in higher estimation than another: all are taught; each has its votaries; and a proper portion of time is allotted to those inferior qualifications, which we every day see assist the greater accomplishments in the acquisition of reputation and fortune. Hence it arises, that the Scotch in general have rather that kind of useful acquaintance with literature, which is so recommended in the *Cortegiano*, as procuring a man friends and esteem; than any great and

deep

deep knowledge in one particular art or language. And hence it is, that we find them excelling the English as Courtiers, and Men of the World; because they are always well stored with such acquisitions as render them more serviceable in society; and from which the most common occasions of life may reap some advantage.

Besides the modern Languages, Music, Painting, Fencing, Riding, and Dancing, are all taught here in some degree of perfection: and manly exercises are admired and encouraged. I remember the celebrated Author whom I before mentioned, makes a skill in wrestling and throwing the coits, and in such other low amusements, absolutely necessary to complete the character of his accomplished Gentleman. On this account, because his grand design being to make himself agreeable, and to be " all things to all men," the method to accomplish this design, was to obtain a knowledge, not only in those things which were useful and profitable, but likewise in those lesser accomplishments which

which have acquired a reputation from the caprice or genius of the different ranks of mankind.

The Royal Academy for Fencing and Riding is always supplied with one of the best masters; who at present is one Angelo Tremermondo, an Italian; and, one would conjecture from his name, from the confines of Mount Vesuvius. The Riding-house is a large and spacious building, admirably adapted to the purpose, and of great benefit to the students: who, in the shortest time possible, have the advantage of taking these wholesome exercises. It is particularly necessary in this City, as the riding on the roads about Edinburgh is exceedingly disagreeable and inconvenient: as they are all paved like the *Pavée* in France, and no part left for the horses on each side. The inhabitants of the City are obliged to drive or ride on the sands at Leith, or Musleborough; which are at least three miles distant, and too far for the young candidate for literary fame constantly to frequent; as it would exhaust too much of his time
from

from recreations of more important consequence.

As I am on the subject of Riding, I must just make one observation, that the Scotch are exceedingly ignorant of horses, and the care and management of them. They have no idea of any thing beyond a Galloway or a strong, slow cart-horse; and what they look on as hunters, are little better. The thorough-bred, sinewy racer, which is now so common in England, is here a phænomenon. They have no genius or taste for riding, nor is it at all encouraged, except in the *Manege*. It is true, indeed, their country is but ill-suited to hunting; which is the reason that it is not worth while breeding that species of horse; and since their principal races are on the sands, on which four miles are equivalent to five on the turf, speed must always yield the victory to strength.

The Scotch are more fond of fencing than riding, and in general excel in it. But their greatest talent seems to be in acquiring the knowledge of, and speaking foreign languages;

guages; which they do with much greater facility than our countrymen. They read also the Latin after the manner of the French, and other nations on the Continent; in which they find much advantage in travelling, as they can be always underſtood, if they are at a loſs to explain themſelves in the language of the country.

There are few of the middle rank of men in this nation but what are in ſome degree acquainted with the Latin tongue, as it is taught in almoſt all the common ſchools; and I believe there are ſeveral branches of buſineſs that find the advantage of it, though trade in general does not ſeem to flouriſh amongſt them; and I fear it will ſtill decreaſe, if the cuſtom of emigrating to America continues ſo much in faſhion. I find even now, that Scotland runs every year ſomewhat in debt, by importing ſo much beyond its exportation; which being to be drawn out in coin, will be a certain, ſlow conſumption of the treaſure of the kingdom, unleſs remedied by
ſumptuary

sumptuary laws, or examples for lessening the importation of foreign commodities, or else by industry for increasing the native, which are either consumed at home, or carried abroad. Two of the greatest sources of wealth to this people, is the fishing trade, and the linen; which they ought to promote by every exertion in their power; the one to keep their money at home, the other to bring in more from abroad.

But on the whole, I do not think the natives of this country calculated for trade, not from their education, but from their natural dispositions and abilities. They want that dull and persevering genius, that aversion to nobler pursuits, which is the characteristic of the Dutch nation. They have a certain ambition implanted in their nature to know more, and appear greater in the eye of the world, than is expected from them; and have (I must call it) such a ridiculous respect to family and ancestry, that one may say with propriety, they prefer a man of quality in poverty and rags, to the richest man upon Change in a coach a coach and six. No wonder then that the idea of a tradesman should be disgusting and disagreeable, when almost every one fancies himself above it, because a century ago there was a peerage in his family.

Believe me your most obedient friend,

and humble servant.

LETTER XXVIII.

On their Gardening, and Improvements in Planting, &c.

To William M—— Esq.

Edinburgh, March 29, 1775.

DEAR SIR,

AMONGST the number of improvements which have been encouraged in Great Britain within a few years, there is one which seems to have made as great a progress in this country as in England; I mean, the improvement of taste in Gardening, Parks, Plantations, and Pleasure Grounds, which is now directly opposite to what it was in the times of our fathers and grandfathers. I cannot look back but with astonishment, to find that it ever entered into the mind of man to imagine, that trees clipt into the resemblance of pillars and animals were beautiful or ornamental; and that the stiff formality of a gravel-walk terras, parterres divided into twenty regular figures,

figures, with a Cupid or a Mercury at each corner, and a mixture of fountains, grotto's, summer-houses and stone-steps, in the space, perhaps, of two acres, should be pleasing or agreeable. And yet we find so great a genius as Sir William Temple, not only praising this disposition for a garden, as the most entertaining and delightful, but handing it down to posterity as the compleatest model.

There is no doubt but that the inhabitants of Scotland lie under many disadvantages with respect to climate; and the prodigious north-east winds, which sweep every thing before them near Edinburgh, render it impossible to have fruit in that perfection, as in parts more to the south: but yet their knowledge in Gardening is by no means inferior to their neighbours; and art and fire in some measure make up for natural deficiencies, and the inclemency of their seasons. As to common kitchen-garden vegetables, I know of no place where they are to be had in greater plenty or perfection than here: The soil seems peculiarly favourable to them, and the whole country round Edinburgh is employed for that purpose. The great abundance of potatoes and carrots, which are excellent of their kind, makes it extremely comfortable to the poorer sort of people, who often can get nothing else to support their families during winter. There are also some places a little distant from the City, which by being in a valley have nothing to counteract the genial warmth of the sun, that have such a profusion of strawberries, that I hardly think Switzerland produces them in greater quantities. I am informed likewise, that gooseberries are equally plentiful, and arrive at the same perfection. There are few cherries, except on walls, that have any flavour. Apricots, peaches, and nectarines, are but of an inferior quality. Figs and mulberries are not to be met with; and few sorts of vines will bear any thing. Though there is but one orchard near Edinburgh, and hardly another in the whole country, I cannot say that common pears and apples are so scarce as you would imagine; but good apples are not to be seen.

The little variety of fruit which this climate brings to perfection, is the cause that the inhabitants set any thing on their tables, after dinner, that has the appearance of it; and I have often observed, at the houses of principal people, a plate of small turnips, which they call "Neeps," introduced in the desert, and eat with as much avidity as if they had been fruit of the first perfection. But if the Scotch are deprived, by the nature of their situation, of the enjoyment of natural fruit, they have the best opportunity of furnishing themselves with hot-houses, as well from the cheapness, as from the excellence of their coals; and, in this respect, have the advantage of the rest of Great Britain. There are few gentlemen of any consequence that are not supplied with fruit by this means; and indeed, melons, pines, grapes, and many other sorts, are produced here with great success.

The Botanical or Physic Garden belonging to the College, is perhaps one of the best in Europe. It is large and spacious, and placed in a warm retired situation, between Leith and Edinburgh; where it is little

little expofed to the fury of the blafts. There are many of the moft curious exotic plants; and a neat and elegant apartment is provided for the Profeffor, who reads a courfe of lectures conftantly every year, for the benefit of the ftudents in medicine.

The gentlemen who have feats near Edinburgh, which, from the romantic and diverfified nature of the country, are generally picturefque and beautiful, deferve the higheft commendation, as well for their tafte and judgment in Planting, as for their encouragement in that ufeful and ornamental diverfion. The rebellious fpirit, and unhappy difturbances, which fo long diftracted this nation, and often brought ruin and defolation into the very heart of the kingdom, prevented, in former times, that attention to rural pleafures, and beautifying the face of their country, which our anceftors fo much delighted in, and of which we every day enjoy the advantage and profit.

Except in the parks of fome particular noblemen, there are few oaks that have feen half a century; which Dr. Johnfon, with his ufual candor and good-nature, feems to fpeak
of

of as an opprobrium; as if it was matter of censure to the present generation, that their forefathers neglected to plant them. It would have been much more worthy the pen of so *patriotic* a Writer, to have told the world, how much posterity will be indebted to modern times for future forests and navies: how an almost barren and uncultivated tract of country will, in a few years, exhibit a new creation, which will equally contribute to pleasure and to wealth, through the industry and elegance of the present inheritors.

The soil of most parts of the Lowlands of Scotland is capable of bearing any sort of timber that is common in the woods in England; and if acorns, ashen-keys, and beech-mast, are sown amongst the different sorts of firs, their growth, and the shoots which they make, are incredible, and surpassing expectation. But there is one thing which I wish was more universal, and more practised in this country, especially near the City of Edinburgh; I mean inclosures of a moderate size, round which, instead of walls of stone, they might raise trees and hedges, that in a short time would amply pay them, and reward their trouble by innumerable advantages. At firſt there would be no neceſſity for any thing but what is natural to the climate, than which nothing can be more ornamental, in producing a conſtant ſpring from their perpetual verdure: and though it cannot be ſaid that their appearance is comparable to the green and vernal hue of thoſe which ſhoot out annually, yet ſurely we cannot but admire the Providence of the Deity, who, in recompence for the more lively plants, which require a greater degree of warmth and ſun-ſhine, has beſtowed on the natives of the North an unvaried and unchangeable beauty.

" For my own part, I am peculiarly
" fond of the whole ſpecies of Evergreens,
" and often find great pleaſure amongſt them
" in the moſt uncomfortable ſeaſons of the
" year. There is ſomething unſpeakably chear-
" ful in a ſpot of ground that is covered with
" trees, which ſmile amidſt all the rigors of
" winter, and which give a view of the moſt
" gay ſeaſon, in the midſt of that which is
" moſt

"most dead and melancholy." For this reason, I wish also to recommend to the Scotch to cultivate the Horn-beam and the Holly, which are highly picturesque and of great utility to fences. I need not tell you what a delightful alteration this would make in the prospect of a country, which, in many parts, is wide and extended, without the appearance of vegetation higher above its surface than a blade of corn; where the only object to intercept the view or diversify the scene, is, perhaps, a sheep-fold, or the gloomy entrance of a coal-mine; or where the eye wanders at large with but one idea, till interrupted by the head of some vast and naked mountain.

But from Plantations and Inclosures in those parts of Scotland which would admit of them, (and almost all the arable part certainly would,) other advantages would be derived independantly of their worth, and the pleasure which they would produce; from the increase of vegetation in purifying the air, and dispelling those putrid and noxious vapours, which are frequently wafted here from the Highlands, to the detriment of animal

mal health; and from the shelter and warmth which they would furnish from the winds, which now traverse the country uncontrolled, without any thing to oppose their passage, and too often

"Tear up the sands, and sweep whole plains away."

But as I must have exhausted your patience, I will conclude with subscribing myself

Your's sincerely.

LETTER XXIX.

The Superstition of the Scotch; the Effects of it in general.

To R. D. Esq;

Edinburgh, April 1, 1775.

SIR,

ONE would imagine, from observing the manners of this Country, that the people considered going to church as one of the most essential points of Religion. Pass thro' Edinburgh during the time of service, and you will not meet with a human creature: the streets are silent and solitary; and you would conclude, from the appearance of them, that some epidemical disorder had depopulated the whole City. But the moment prayers are over, the scene changes: they pour from the churches in multitudes, which nothing but having seen can give you any idea of. Even with every care possible you are driven from one side to another, till your shoulders are almost dislocated; for they are

so

so intently employed with meditating on the good things they have heard, and the enjoyments of another life, that they have no time to look before them. They proceed in one uniform pace, with their large prayer-books under their arms, their eyes fixed steadily on the ground, and wrapped up in their plaid cloaks, regardless of every thing that passes. After having remained some time at home, they again sally out to church, where they continue till five o'clock in the evening. At this hour all public devotions are over for the day; and they then begin their little schemes of entertainment. The young Girls, who have been melting in devotion for the space of six or seven hours, take walks in the meadows and other places with their Lovers, in order to amuse themselves: and, what you will probably think very strange, it often happens that this heavenly temper of mind produces effects which are quite the reverse. The older people, whose religion is less enthusiastic, retire to little innocent parties, where the scandal of the town, and the faults of their neighbours, are very piously discussed.

The

The influence of Superstition is ridiculously strong in this country. The Clergy are expected to go to no public place whatever: a Play, in particular, however innocent or sentimental, is esteemed highly immoral for a Minister; and were he once to be seen at an Assembly, he might as well resign his profession; for no one would listen to him afterwards. Deprived of all enjoyment abroad, many of them seek it at home in a bottle; for they know that " wine maketh man of " a chearful countenance." Were it not for this consolation (of which many of them drink very deep) they would really pass the most unsociable life that can be imagined. Watched and observed every where, all the common indulgences of living denied to them, liable to be deprived of their office for the slightest offences, they are only rewarded for all this mortification by an income of one hundred pounds a year, and many of them by a much smaller sum.

During the Lent season they have a particular week, which is called, very properly, *the preaching week*; for they really do nothing but pray. This week is distinguished by
every

every method of folemnity; and every perfon is expected to attend church conftantly. The Sacrament is adminiftered at this time; and it is thought highly indecent not to receive it. All the people of fafhion wait for this week before they retire into the country: for in fome meafure it anfwers the purpofes of confeffion; and they are enabled to pafs the remaining part of the year with chearfulnefs and eafe. All is conducted in a very regular way. The Clergy rail at the people for the ungodlinefs of the paft winter: the people repent, and are forgiven, till the next year obliges them to afk a frefh pardon for frefh offences.

I think I need fcarcely obferve to you, that in fpite of this outward fhew, and the force of fuperftition, that the Scotch, as a nation, are far from being religious: Deifm is the ruling principle. Shocked with the grofs abfurdities with which their religion is loaded, they pay an obedience to it externally, but treat it with very little ceremony in private. In fome meafure this is the natural confequence. The mind, revolting at the folly and inconfiftencies with which priefts

in

in the anxiety of their zeal perplex the fyftem, too frequently runs into the other extreme; and, convinced of the improbability of many points of faith, becomes an infidel in all.

It is a maxim, which is but too true, that the corruption of the beft things terminates in the worft. How frequently has many a good and moral man renounced all the bleffings which religion offers to mankind, rather than give his affent to what is marked with ignorance or cruelty!

The French, who long laboured under the fevereft of all flaveries in that point, and who were amufed with the wonderful power of certain little pieces of wood in the fhape of croffes, and a long train of other abfurdities, are now become unbelievers by profeffion; and, being convinced what a farce has been impofed upon them under the name of Religion, are now unhappily led to imagine, that the thing itfelf is a farce.

How happy are the Proteftants, but particularly the Englifh, in being free from thofe abfurd prejudices which fo long fubjected the human mind; and which, in many countries,

enflave

enflave it to this day! How happy ought we to be in having at laft eftablifhed a fyftem which fupports itfelf by its own fimplicity, and the purity of its profeffors! where the duties it prefcribes are calm and rational; and where its firft obligation is that of making a man a good citizen in the fociety in which he is placed; and which unites the neceffity of good actions to the doctrine of belief!

Though the religion of this Country, like our own, preaches Meeknefs and Charity, yet it is too much employed in the obfervance of little trivial folemnities, which are, in reality, of no moment: for an attention to every petty circumftance in life detaches the mind from all the more important duties of morality.

I own, that with every poffible refpect for Religion, and which every man ought to feel, I read its hiftory with aftonifhment. Inftead of being a detail of peace and humility, which it would naturally feem to infpire, it is nothing but a collection of wars, impiety, and murder: cruel and wicked men triumphant; the good infulted, and frequently fuffering an ignominious death; every fpecies of torment invented for them, under the name

of

of religion; fires kept alive by the bodies of those that were cast into them: and streets streaming with the blood of people, charged with no other crime than thinking differently from ourselves.

"The proper office of Religion," says Mr. Hume in his History of England, "is
"to reform men's lives, to purify their hearts,
"to enforce all moral duties, and to secure
"obedience to the laws and civil magistrate.
"While it pursues these salutary purposes,
"its operations, though infinitely valuable,
"are secret and silent. It is that adulterate
"species of it alone, which inflames faction,
"which animates sedition, and prompts to
"every thing that is corrupt and wicked."

If this is the case, what probity of heart, as well as gentleness of manners, ought those men to possess who explain and enforce its doctrines in the several Countries where they are educated, and undertake that profession? Can one be so much astonished at that general system of infidelity which seems now prevailing so fast, when one reads the enormous crimes of which some of the Professors of Christianity have been guilty, and which they have profanely sanctified by the name of Religion?

In turning over an old Italian author I found the following story, which is a strong example of what I advance: A Nobleman of great interest in Portugal, had married a very beautiful Lady, of whom he was passionately fond. In some revolutions of the Church, which were then talked of, the Jesuits found it necessary to secure this Nobleman to their Party. A *Religieux* was, therefore, dispatched into the family; who, by a number of different arts, insinuated himself into the good graces of the Lady. The Husband, who imagined that his visits were entirely on the part of Religion, paid little attention to them. A Brother, however, of the Lady's, and an officer, began to suspect that something more than Religion might be the subject of these interviews; and on entering her apartment one day, he surprised the Lady and the holy Father in circumstances not the least equivocal. At such an interruption, and in such circumstances, the Lady screamed, and fainted away: the Officer advanced, and drew his sword; but the Father, neither
abashed

abashed by the situation in which he had been discovered, nor intimidated by the action of the Brother, advanced towards him, "Wretch!" cried he, "how darest thou thus "pry into the holy secrets of the Church, "and not dread the just vengeance of the "Inquisition?" At these tremendous words the Officer dropt the point of his sword.— "Well mayest thou be afraid," pursued the Father, "for thy impudence calls aloud for "punishment. But go: I forgive thee. Do "not, however, imagine that I have enjoyed "thy Sister out of any carnal desires: No; "Heaven knows the uprightness of my "heart; and that the Professors of Religion "are pure. The Church had occasion for "thy Brother, but he was obstinate: I took, "therefore, the means of this tender Lamb," pointing to the Lady, "who has an interest "with her Husband, to effect our gracious "and pious purposes."

I have the honour to be, &c.

LETTER XXX.

On the Ridotto.

To Miss Lucinda B——

Edinburgh, April 6, 1775.

MY DEAR LUCINDA,

I Must beg leave to break in upon your more agreeable avocations for a moment, to acquaint you that we have had a Ridotto here.

The Manager of the Theatre had at the first proposed introducing a Masquerade: a species of entertainment hitherto unknown in a public style.

A Gentleman, indeed, attempted a private Masquerade at his own house last year; but, I am informed, he by no means succeeded, for want of a proper variety of company, and their not understanding the nature and spirit of the diversion. But this was no reason with Mr. Digges why a general one in so large and public a place as as the Theatre, should not stand a better chance of succeeding, than the select number of friends of any particular person. He, therefore, with the laudable intention of introducing a Masquerade, which, of all other Amusements, is of the greatest utility to trade and manufactories, declared his resolution, and fixed the evening of the entertainment: well knowing, could he once prevail on the inhabitants of the City to attend, a little experience and practice would soon give them a taste for it; and one only in a season would be no unacceptable addition to the profits of the Play-house.

Thus it continued a little time, apparently in a likely road to success: but for want of some of the principal people to patronize it, he at last perceived it would be impossible to have it in that fashionable and polite manner he could have wished; and therefore prudently changed the Masquerade to a *Ridotto*; which I hope has out-done his most ardent expectations in point of profit, as his proper behaviour calls on every degree of testimony to his desert.

But there was another reason why a Masquerade did not take place: Presbyterianism and the Kirk, those formidable enemies to Mirth and Jollity, pronounced their *anathema*; and every argument was mustered up in opposition to it, that could be brought against Immorality, Vice, and the Devil. I am not certain whether it was absolutely forbid from the Pulpit; but it is most probable it was, as the private masquerade became the subject of many a sermon, and was thundered against as the encourager of Intrigue, of Libertinism, of Debauchery. Yet, so great is the power of prejudice, that, notwithstanding the same objections might have been made with equal propriety against a Ridotto, or, indeed, any other public amusement, not one word was spoken in disapprobation; but every one united in commendation of Mr. Digges for changing it, and rejoiced, as if he had been the " one Sinner that repented."

Well, the long-expected evening arrived; the tickets were a guinea: and the whole Fashionable World of Edinburgh were assembled; some to discountenance Masquerades, others to countenance Ridotto's, and the

the reft to pafs the evening in any agreeable manner that the place afforded, not materially concerning themfelves what entertainment it was, fo that Pleafure, the darling object of the mind, the difpeller of care, melancholy, and that *ennui*, which makes life itfelf fo burden-fome, was fome-how or other to be obtained. Among the firft tribe were the religious of all forts and determinations, from the Minifter's wife and daughter, to the antiquated Maid of fifty-fix — who, having paffed the grand climacteric of virginity, together with her defire for mankind, pretended an abhorrence of a recreation that might be productive of fo many confequences; either through envy at the rifing generation of upftart miffes, left they fhould be more fuccefsful than fhe had been; or elfe, through the remembrance of the advantage fhe would have taken of fuch an occafion, in days of yore,

" Before Polygamy was held a Sin."

Of the middle clafs were thofe who loved either diverfion, but having purchafed the

annual

annual *negligée* or dressed coat, thought the Ridotto best adapted to the œconomy of their pocket; and that the encouragement of trade was an inferior consideration to the discouragement of their own finances.

Of the last order were the Beaux, Belles, Coxcombs, and Coquettes, the jovial Votaries of Revelry and Good Humour, and all those indolent mortals, whose greatest torment is to stay at home, though too idle to leave it without regret.

> Thee too, my M——, I saw thee there
> Stretch'd on the rack of a too easy chair;
> And heard thy everlasting groan confess
> The pains and penalties of Idleness.

The Pit was covered over after the manner of the Opera House in London on a like occasion. The Side-boxes were converted into reservoirs of wines, ices, and every kind of refreshment: and at the upper end of the stage was an Orchestra of all the principal Musicians, both vocal and instrumental; who, after the company had been assembled a short time, displayed their several abilities, and performed

performed some pieces adapted to the purpose.

The ornaments and decorations of the other parts of the Theatre were with equal propriety, taste, and elegance. Over the boxes were the illuminated heads of the Poets, after whose names the boxes are denominated, and over the stage boxes, landscapes done in the same form, by Runciman, the Sir Joshua Reynolds of this country, and whose invention is perhaps equal to that of any painter in Europe.

The ball began with minuets danced in different parts of the room, which lasted but a short time, and then gave place to the more enlivening harmony of a country-dance; after a certain interval, an orchestra afforded entertainment to the company during the time of administering refreshments. The night was closed by the addition of French horns and clarinets, which the Gentlemen of the regiment, who were quartered here, politely provided.

You will wonder to hear me say, that, notwithstanding there was the greatest profusion

sion of excellent wines, not one person attempted to stay after the departure of the Ladies, and not a single glass fell a victim to excess. In this respect, the Scotch Gentlemen contradicted themselves, and with an uncommon degree of prudence and regularity, endeavoured to make the entertainment as profitable as possible to the manager, who had exerted himself to please them, and who justly had merited the general approbation.

I am sensible, after all this, you wait with expectation to hear my partner; but for once, you must excuse my saying any thing more, than that she was handsome, extremely polite, and a good dancer. But suffer me to assure you, that however prevalent may be the power of Scotch beauty, however captivating the roseate hue, the dimpled cheek, and sparkling eye of the virgins of the North; my heart is still impenetrable, whilst the image of Lucinda, like my guardian angel, presents itself to all other allurements, and breaks the inchantment of every other beauty. No, my Lucinda, object of all
my

my hopes; happiness has but half its value without your participation. The Ridotto wanted nothing but you, to make it completely agreeable, and that defect diminished all its pleasures, to

Your ever sincere and affectionate friend.

LETTER XXXI.

On the Gallantry and Politeness of the Scotch, their Intrigues, &c.

To R. D. Esq.

Edinburgh, April 12, 1775.

DEAR SIR,

THAT imperious and disgusting character, which always arrogates to itself alone Reason and Sense, and will not allow any one else to possess them, and be in the right, I never saw in this country; and I think there is no better sign of a perfectly well-bred man, than the appearance of diffidence, with the possession of knowledge, and the giving every possible attention to the judgment and opinion of others.

The Scotch Gentlemen, in their families, at their tables, or in company, have a certain plausible civility and complaisance, which give them the appearance of virtue,

and

and make them on the outside, what men in general ought to be within. They always seem pleased with you, and converse on subjects with which you are most acquainted, so that their guest leaves them well-pleased with himself, and consequently with them. They entertain their visitors with the highest degree of courtesy, without compliment, or formality, and rather choose to listen to the sentiments of others, than give their own opinion in a general company. *I pensieri stretti et il volto sciolto*, is the Delphian oracle, which seems to be ever in their memory.

The Scotch Ladies also are peculiarly attentive in their own houses, and discharge the duties of their families with much ease, œconomy, and politeness. At their tables, they share with their husbands the greatest assiduity to entertain, and shew more desire to make every thing free from ceremony, than in any nation with which I have yet been conversant. The men, in general, are neither disposed for Gallantry, nor formed for it, from their education or temper. They rather pay too little attention to the Ladies, which is partly occasioned cafioned by habit, partly by their genius. Notwithftanding, they affociate together more, perhaps, than in fome other countries; you feldom fee a Scotchman putting himfelf to an inconvenience to accommodate or find in him any anxiety to pleafe the other fex.

The feverity of the laws of Scotland with refpect to marriage, and promifes relating to it, feem to keep the young men under a reftraint, and hinder them from making ufe of the moft innocent freedoms, which every where elfe are expected by the Ladies. A lover in Scotland is the moft ignorant Thing imaginable; I mean as to addrefs, compliments, proteftations, and endearments, which are fo familiar in the mouths of an Englifh *inamorato*—In true love indeed,

> " E'l filentio ancor fuole
> " Aver prieghi & parole."

or elfe I do not know how they would communicate their paffion.

Their tafte in beauty is not very exquifite, though they have the fineft models in the world. Large women pleafe them moft, most, and they pay little regard to a just symmetry of parts, complexion, or colour. The eyes are the charm which attracts them most, and whose language they best understand.

But the women are of a different nature and disposition from the men. They are all freedom, all affability, and breathe the very spirit of Gallantry. They have a certain vivacity and negligence in their behaviour, which has the most amiable appearance you can conceive. The most enchanting looks, and all the allurements of the Cyprian Queen, seem to be their inheritance; which, perhaps, are rather increased than diminished by the deficiency of inflammability in the men. To rouse the latent spark, every assistance is necessary, so that it is their interest to be perfect mistresses in the art of pleasing; and indeed, they are arrived at such perfection in it, as to be excelled by none in Europe.

But I am happy to tell you, that that abandoned spirit for Intrigue, which is so predominant in our country, is as yet a perfect stranger to these northern climes. No people

people are more conſtant, faithful and ſincere in their amours; and though the married may ſometimes have the appearance of levity and wantonneſs, it is occaſioned by the liberty and mode of their education. The name of adultery is hardly known; it is a *rara avis*, a phœnix which exiſts only once in a hundred years.

You would imagine at firſt the young women the leaſt fortified againſt the aſſaults of libertiniſm and licentiouſneſs, ſo familiar and unguarded ſeems their manner of intercourſe with the men: but it is quite otherwiſe; ſo far from expoſing them, it is their ſtrongeſt defence. They acquire an effrontery and method of arguing, that baffle the ſeducer, and by the ſeeming loſs of it, ſecure their innocence. During the whole time that I have been in Edinburgh, there has been but one inſtance of a falſe ſtep having been made by a young lady of any kind of family or faſhion; and it ſeems Eudocia had received her education in England. She was extremely young, having juſt entered into her fifteenth year, when ſhe was brought down hither by her father, a true Highland

Highland Laird, who fancied that his daughter poſſeſſed every female accompliſhment; and that it was high time to form a connection with one of the quality of his own country. A natural vivacity of fancy, accompanied with an agreeable ſoftneſs of diſpoſition, rendered her as much the admiration of thoſe who converſed with her, as a genteel figure, and delicate complexion, gained her the adoration of thoſe who ſaw her. The retirement of a London Boarding-ſchool, and the romantic notions ſhe had imbibed from books which ſhe had been permitted to read there, gave her ſuch a taſte for amuſement and the faſhionable pleaſures of company, that, on every occaſion, Eudocia was a principal party. Was there a public aſſembly? ſhe was preſent. Was there a play? you were ſure to find her in the ſtage box: nor was ſhe to be ſeen leſs frequent in the public walks, than at the kirk. Wherever ſhe appeared, ſhe became the envy of the women, and admiration of the men; whom ſhe attracted by her charms, who were ambitious of her attention, and aſſiduous

assiduous of approving themselves worthy of paying her civilities.

Among the crowd of her followers was Bellario: who soon conceived an affection, though at first his addresses were only the effect of fashion, and the desire of conformity of taste with the rest of his acquaintance. His figure, his wit, his education, temper, every thing conspired to fit him for the conquest of the most guarded virtue.

After, therefore, walking in private, dancing with her, and exciting her love and inclination, by all the arts which experience had taught him to triumph over the unfortunate victims of his desire, he at length prevailed on her to admit him by moonlight into her chamber window, where every thing crowned his ambition, and

 Cupid smil'd to see his shafts so sure.

Vanity, on one side, and that regard which a woman always discovers for the object who has deprived her of the most valuable possession, soon discovered their intercourse, and rendered their amour the topic of public conversation. Manifest signs also of her indiscretion,

discretion, made it absolutely necessary for Bellario to remove her from her father's house, who for some time had harboured suspicions, and was just on the verge of demanding an explanation concerning his intimacy with Eudocia. At length some lucky opportunity favoured their elopement, and she was conveyed to a private lodging in London, where her paramour, soon satisfied by perpetual enjoyment, found satiety an antidote for his passion; and after a short time abandoned her to the world, deprived of a father, a friend, of every thing. The little pittance she had saved from her seducer, served but a short time to supply her necessities, till she determined to return back to Edinburgh, where she hoped for some compassion from her former acquaintance. But alas! the loss of virtue and distress are sure to attend each other. A parent deaf to every intreaty; her female associates ridiculing her misfortunes; whilst the unfaithful herd of her former admirers, who once would have died at her frown, now unpitying and unmoved, behold her misery with contempt. After a short interval, being destitute

tute even of advice, and hardened by the cruelty of those, whose compassion only she intreated, Eudocia was insnared by the pretended friendship of a mistress of a brothel; where a continued scene of vice is now so familiar to her, that her charms are prostituted to every lustful ruffian, who has money to pay the wages of her iniquity.

I have dwelt thus long on this history, because I know you esteem Bellario as your friend; but I hope, for the future, you will consider no man in that light, who can thus forfeit his pretensions to honour and humanity. I have often been surprised, that even the common feelings of the heart, the sympathy that we have for our fellow-creatures, have not been able to deter these assassins of innocence, though destitute of virtue, and dead to the dictates of conscience.

Happy would the world be, if instances of this kind were as seldom in other places, as in this City. Intriguing in Edinburgh is not understood: the men have no talent for it; as well from their education as their genius. I wish I could say as much for our own countrymen. But in England every day

day is conscious of a new Intrigue; which is not only bad from the evil it produces, but from the crimes it naturally supposes antecedent to it. Fraud, dissimulation, and perjury, are the instruments of an Intrigue; and such instruments are not thrown away when they have served one occasion, but are laid by for other opportunities. For the same depravity, which will lead a man to be the cause of misery, shame, and affliction to a whole family, to bring with sorrow to the grave disconsolate parents, and murder with infamy the character of her he once loved, will equally induce him, where interest is concerned, to betray his brother, or sacrifice his friend.

I have the honour to be, &c.

LETTER XXXII.

On the Scotch Dances.

To Mrs. F———r, at Bath.

Edinburgh, April 20, 1775.

DEAR MADAM,

IF you have been informed the Scotch dance well, I beg that you will retain your favourable opinion of them, without asking mine; for, on this point, I am by no means partial to them. The Dances of this country are entirely void of grace; which appears to me to be the first principle, unless we consider it, as the Savages do, merely as an exercise.

The general Dance here is a Reel, which requires that particular sort of step to dance properly, of which none but people of the country can have any idea. All the English whom I have seen attempt it, were very deficient in their imitations; and though the Scotch were too polite openly to laugh at them, they saw and felt the ridicule of grown gentlemen learning to dance.

The

The perseverance which the Scotch Ladies discover in these Reels, is not less surprising, than their attachment to them in preference to all others. They will sit totally unmoved at the most sprightly airs of an English Country Dance; but the moment one of these tunes is played, which is liquid laudanum to my spirits, up they start, animated with new life, and you would imagine they had received an electrical shock, or been bit by a tarantula. A Lady, who, for half an hour before, has sat groaning under the weight of a large hoop and a corpulent habit of body, the instant one of these tunes is applied to her ear, shall bounce off her seat, and frisk and fly about the room to the great satisfaction of all the spectators.

These tunes were originally performed on the bagpipe: but you will naturally be surprised how so drowsy an instrument should be capable of inspiring such uncommon ardour. The effect which these national Dances have, and the partiality which many nations discover for them, is certainly

certainly matter of great surprise to a stranger. An ingenious writer says, "That the "fury and violence which the Spaniards dis- "cover in dancing the Fandango, the ori- "ginal Dance of their country, can only be "compared to the fire and eagerness of the "Italian horses before the barrier is let down "for their running." This violence, making an allowance for the different heat of the different climates, is equally discoverable in the Scotch.

The young people in England, you know, only consider Dancing as an agreeable means of bringing them together; and, was not gallantry to be of the party, I am afraid we should most of us think it a very stupid sort of a meeting. But the Scotch admire the Reel for its own merit alone, and may truly be said to dance for the sake of Dancing. I have often sat a very wearied spectator of one of these Dances, in which not one graceful movement is seen, the same invariably, if continued for hours. How different is this from the *Allemande!* A Scotchman comes into an assembly-room as

he

he would into a field of exercife, dances till he is literally tired, poffibly without ever looking at his partner, or almoft knowing who he dances with. In moft countries the men have a partiality for dancing with a woman; but here I have frequently feen four gentlemen perform one of thefe Reels feemingly with the fame pleafure and perfeverance as they would have done, had they had the moft fprightly girl for a partner. The Reel is the only thing which gives them pleafure: if the figure is formed, it appears, no matter with what; and they give you the idea, that they could, with equal glee, caft off round a joint ftool, or fet to a corner cupboard.

Another of the national Dances is a kind of quick minuet, or what the Scotch call a *Strafpae*. We in England are faid to *walk* a minuet: this is gallopping a minuet. The French one is efteemed by all the people at the Opera, as peculiarly elegant, and affording the greateft opportunity poffible for a fine woman to difplay her figure to advantage. In this of the Scotch, however, every idea of

grace

grace seems inverted, and the whole is a burlesque: nothing of the minuet is preserved, except the figure; the step and the time most resemble an hornpipe — and I leave you to dwell upon the picture of a gentleman full-dressed, and a lady in an hoop, lappets, and every other incumbrance of ornament, dancing an hornpipe before a large assembly.

To those who may be fond of these dances, what I have said will be called prejudice. I flatter myself you will not think so: for I should esteem myself infinitely below your regard, could I be carried away by so ridiculous a passion upon any subject, much less upon such an one as this; where one may truly say, " *Le Jeu ne vaut pas la Chandelle.*" But without any partiality to our own, or any other country, I shall not hesitate to say, the Scotch dance more ungracefully than any other people I have yet seen. The Swifs, who are far from being a refined or polished nation, dance naturally, in the most graceful style imaginable: two young peasants, with no other ornaments but chearful, healthy looks, and

and sprightly countenances, shall discover, in a little rural *Allemande*, as many expressive and striking attitudes, as many fine inclinations of figure, as would be applauded on a stage. The Scotch, however, have nothing but their enthusiasm and activity to recommend them. It is no civility to attempt to shew them any thing new: they hold their dances sacred, and will bear no innovation on that point. Cotillons, and other French dances, have not travelled so far north—And you may tell them (for I suppose you are at present in the midst of them) that they might as well stay where they are.

The Ladies, however, to do them justice, dance much better than the men. But I once had the honour of being witness to a reel in the Highlands, where the party consisted of three maiden ladies, the youngest of whom was above fifty, which was conducted with gestures so uncouth, and a vivacity so hideous, that you would have thought they were acting some midnight ceremonies, or enchanting the moon.

The graveſt men here, with the exception of the miniſters, think it no diſgrace to dance. I have ſeen a profeſſor, who has argued moſt learnedly and moſt wiſely in a morning, forgetting all his gravity in an evening, and dance away to the beſt of his abilities.

The lower claſs of people here are as fond of dancing as their betters: they have their little parties and private rooms, where they indulge themſelves in this pleaſure; and frequently, when the labours and the fatigues of the day are over, they refreſh themſelves by a Dance. This is an odd cuſtom: but they are not ſingular in it; a French Peaſant does juſt the ſame.

I have exceeded the uſual bounds of a letter, and it is full time to put an end to this. I am much afraid (to uſe a common expreſſion) ' that I have led you ſuch a dance,' you will not wiſh to hear from me again ſoon. I owe you more than I can expreſs to you, when I remember that, in the midſt of gaiety and diverſion, and ſurrounded by admirers,

mirers, you could find time to cast a thought upon a man who is at present four hundred miles from you. If I can be happy enough in future to give you any information on subjects more calculated to entertain you, it will, in reality, be conferring a pleasure on me, in the opportunity it will afford me of perusing your letters.

I have the honour to be, Dear Madam, &c.

LETTER

LETTER XXXIII.

The Climate, and its Influence.

To R. D. Esq.

Edinburgh, April 25, 1775.

SIR,

I Have hitherto delayed giving you any account of the climate of this Country, as I was resolved to wait till I could send you an opinion of my own, or at least form some judgment of the truth of that of others.

The natives of this Country, who have travelled much into warmer climates, tell you, that Scotland is far colder than England, and that you cannot clothe yourself too warmly in winter. As to myself, I have not as yet found any of these precautions necessary, and I wear just the same number of cloaths I should do in England at this season of the year.

Though this winter has hitherto been very mild,

mild, I can easily perceive that the weather is much more changeable than it is in England, and that frequently you experience all the seasons in one day. In the middle of it, when the Sun is in his meridian, the heat is sometimes extremely powerful; and in the evening you have all that piercing cold you might expect here in winter. From these reasons the Medical People say, that it is the worst climate in the world for the use of mercurial medicines; that in very few constitutions they have any effect; and that in many they are entirely fatal. I have been assured from the best authority, that in many venereal cases the proper remedies are impracticable, and that it has been frequently found necessary to remove the patient to England, in order to establish a cure. It is probably to be attributed to this cause, that they have in Scotland, a disorder which they call the "*Sibbens,*" and which is a compound of the Scotch and venereal disease that has hitherto baffled all the aids of medicine. Its consequences are the most baneful that can be conceived, as it

gradually

gradually deftroys every part of the human frame, before it puts an end to life; and, if what I am told is true, it is ftill more dreadful—as it is to be caught by merely touching an infected perfon, and not in the manner of the common venereal diforder.

The moft particular effect which I find of this Climate, is the Winds; which here reign in all their violence, and feem indeed to claim the country as their own. A perfon, who has paffed all his time in England, cannot be faid to know what a wind is: he has zephyrs, and breezes, and gales, but nothing more; at leaft they appear fo to me after having felt the hurricanes of Scotland.

As this Town is fituated on the borders of the fea, and furrounded by hills of an immenfe height, the currents of air are carried down between them with a rapidity and a violence which nothing can refift. It has frequently been known, that in the New Town at Edinburgh three or four people have fcarce been able to fhut the door of the houfe; and it is a very common accident to hear of fedan chairs

chairs being overturned. It seems almost a necessary compliment here, to wait upon a lady the next morning, to hope she got safe home. In many visits which I have made since I came here, two people have been obliged to go on each side of the chair, to keep it even while other two have carried it; and sometimes even this precaution has not been sufficient. Not many days ago an Officer, whom I have the honour of being acquainted with, a man of six feet high, and, one would imagine, by no means calculated to become the sport of winds, was, however, in following another gentleman out of the Castle, lifted up by their violence from the ground, carried over his companion's head, and thrown at some distance on the stones. This, I can assure you, is a literal fact.

At other times, the winds, instead of rushing down with impetuosity, whirl about in eddies, and become still more dreadful. On these occasions it is almost impossible to stir out of doors, as the dust and stones gathered up in these vortices not only prevent your seeing, but frequently cut your legs by the velocity with which they are driven. The Scotch have a particular appellation for this, "*The Stour.*"

The chief scene where these winds exert their influence, is the New Bridge, which, by being thrown over a long valley that is open at both ends, and particularly from being ballustraded on each side, admits the wind in the most charming manner imaginable; and you receive it with the same force you would do, were it conveyed to you through a pair of bellows. It is far from unentertaining for a man to pass over this bridge on a tempestuous day. In walking over it this morning I had the pleasure of adjusting a lady's petticoats which had blown almost entirely over her head, and which prevented her disengaging herself from the situation she was in: but in charity to her distresses, I concealed her charms from public view: one poor gentleman, who was rather too much engaged with the novelty of the objects before him, unfortunately forgot his own hat and wig, which were lifted up by an unpremeditated

unpremeditated puff, and carried entirely away.

But though the bleak air of this Climate may give, as it is said to do, that keen and penetrating look to the inhabitants, which they certainly possess, as well as great activity of body, they are far from being healthy in general. I have scarce met with one instance of remarkable longevity amongst all the people I have seen, and there are very few places where you observe more funerals. Whether this is to be attributed entirely to the climate, or in some part to the College of Physicians, who are very eminent in their profession, I leave you to determine for yourself.

There is one circumstance here which certainly deserves notice, as it is a contradiction to all the rules which are laid down in regard to climates; I mean, the early maturity of their women. It is generally imagined that cold has the same degree of influence over the animal, as it has over the vegetable world; but in this country they are in direct opposition; for the plants are very late, and the girls extremely forward.

In reading Mr. Wraxall's Account of Sweden the other day, I found an obfervation of the fame kind, which he attributes to their conftantly bathing in warm baths during the winter time; but then he remarks, they want that firmnefs of flefh, that elafticity which is fo defirable to an Englifhman, and of which, indeed, this young Author complains with great feeling.

I imagine, however, that the early maturity of the Scotch girls cannot be attributed to the fame caufe. Many of the ladies marry at fifteen; and many of the married ladies at twenty-five, look no younger than fome of the Englifh women at forty. This early lofs of beauty may, in fome meafure, proceed from a negligence of their perfons the moment they are married, as if, on that important day, all future defires of pleafing were to be clofed, and one dark cloud of conftancy and indifference was to fhade the whole fcene.

In regard to the productions of the earth, this Country is certainly later than any part of England by fome weeks; and in the Highlands a great quantity of the corn never ripens upon the ground, but is cut wet and unripe, and dried by being hung up under cover.

Notwithstanding all the care that can be taken, very little fruit is to be got here; and indeed the very best is so bad, that it is scarce worth the rearing. As they have no Spring in this Climate, nothing of what the Italians express by the *Gioventu' del anno*, all the blossoms are either destroyed by the frosts, or the ripening is thrown so late in the season, that the succeeding Winter sweeps them away before they can arrive at any perfection. In the month of May, which, in the Southern parts of England, is frequently the most agreeable month in the whole year, they have here certain winds, which blow from a particular quarter sometimes during the whole month, and answer, in some measure, to the *trade winds*, which render it, as I am informed, the most disagreeable month in the year. The fine weather is seldom entirely formed till the beginning or the middle of July, and continues till the end of October;

the remaining months all pafs under the denomination of winter. They feem to have only two feafons, Summer and Winter; as frequently the moft fultry weather immediately fucceeds to the coldeft and moft tempeftuous.

I mean to trouble you with only one obfervation more, with which a perfon muft be ftruck in every part of this Country, and which they attribute to the Climate—it is the extreme uglinefs of all the common people. How often have we heard air and exercife recommended as the only prefervatives of beauty! How often have the Poets carried us back to the charms and the graces, and I know not what, of former ages, when people paffed their whole lives in the open air? How often are we ferioufly told, by moralifts, to look for beautiful perfons amongft peafants, and not in the artificial fplendor of a drawing-room, or the counterfeit brilliancy of a court! I only wifh, that all thefe pretty declaimers would take a fhort excurfion into this Country, to be convinced how idle all their fuppofitions are: they would find a

country

country in which temperance and labour are in the extreme; and where, inſtead of ruddy cheeks, ſprightly countenances, and graceful figures, they would behold haggard looks, meagre complexions, and bodies that are weakened by fatigue, and worn down by the inclemency of the ſeaſons.

I have the honour to be, &c.

LETTER XXXIV.

Funerals, and the Mode of conducting them.

To R. D. Efq;

Edinburgh, April 28, 1775.

SIR,

I Know no place where you behold more frequent Funerals than in this City, and they are conducted with a filence and a folemnity which makes forrow appear ftill more difmal. On thefe occafions, in England, you know, no diftrefs is feen; for, as the afflicted hire others to mourn for them, it cannot be fuppofed that people fhould be affected by diftreffes which are nothing to them. An Englifhman feems to carry with him the fame defires out of life, which he had in it; and as all his pleafure was centered in going poft, you frequently meet his hearfe at a full gallop, as if, after having been in an hurry all his lifetime, it was decreed he fhould find no reft even in death.

In this place, instead of applying to an undertaker for a groupe of grim figures, and dismal faces, they send a card, as the French do, to all the persons of their acquaintance, desiring their attendance at the Funeral. If the people who are invited do not really feel sorrow in compliment at least they affect to do so; and therefore, you are not shocked with any ill-timed mirth or outward signs of insensibility. They all dress themselves at these meetings in a suit of black, which has something in it peculiarly mournful: all the nearest relations, besides putting on weepers, which are common with us, fix a long piece of muslin to the collar of the shirt, that hangs down before as far as the middle of the waist. They continue this fashion all the time they wear their first mourning, and sometimes the excess of their grief is in proportion to these pieces of muslin.

In the Funerals of the lower classes of people, the procession is always on foot. The coffin is carried by four people, the minister walks before it, and all the friends and relations follow. They proceed with a slow, solemn

solemn pace to the Kirk: and as the relationship extends itself a great way in this Country, a whole street is sometimes nearly filled with this sable procession.

Persons of higher rank are carried in hearses; but with none of that ostentatious pomp and ceremony which is so frequent, and generally so ridiculous in England. The vanity of people in this Country dies with them. You are never astonished with a display of which they can be no longer sensible, and from whence no gratification can be derived, but one of the most melancholy and disgusting nature: an hearse, followed by a mourning coach, is all the parade that you see; and if a man has done nothing in life worth remembering, he has no chance of making himself immortal by his Funeral. The undertakers seem the only people who suffer by all this humility; they neither find people to mourn, nor plumes of feathers, nor carriages, nor any of those *insignia mortis*, which few people would think of having, could they only see the bill.

There is one instance of politeness which the Scotch shew each other, and which, as

for

far as mere ceremonial can be agreeable, is certainly so: whenever a relation of any family dies, the first visit made to them by their friends and even acquaintances, is always made in mourning, as if to sympathise with their distress. This piece of form they observe with great care; and a person would be thought a strange creature who should go dressed in colours to the house of mourning. This custom is never repeated. From these civilities, and the frequent mournings which the numerous relationship occasion, many families are almost constantly cloathed in black; and on entering a large room full of company, one would sometimes imagine that an epidemical disorder was raging in the Town, and that every one of them had lost some near relation. But whether it is from the constant habit of mourning that the occasion of it loses in some measure its effect, or that they are a nation of philosophers, they do not appear to me to feel with all that lively and tender sensibility, which is visible in some countries. They weep for a little time, they then begin to think of something fashionable for a mourning

ing drefs, and every thing goes on as before. The widows, indeed, put on fo very forrowful an appearance, and wrap themfelves fo entirely in black, that one would imagine they had devoted the reft of their lives to melancholy, and never intended to take another hufband. But yet, in fpite of all this, many of them do, and " mourn their " loves like the Dame of Ephefus." I remember reading a ftory, which is far from being a bad comment on thefe extravagant ladies: For want of fomething better, I will conclude this letter with it.

" An Indian woman came to the gover-
" nor of the town where fhe lived, and told
" him, that as her hufband was dead, fhe
" hoped he would give her leave to burn
" herfelf alive, according to the cuftom of her
" country. The governor, who had long
" endeavoured to difcourage thefe practices,
" refufed to grant her requeft. ' How!' cried
" the woman, ' not burn myfelf! here is a
" governor for you indeed! A poor widow
" only afks leave to burn herfelf for the
" good of the public, and fhe cannot obtain
" permiffion to do fo! My mother, my
                                " aunts,

"aunts, and my sisters all burnt themselves
"in a creditable manner, and here, unfor-
"tunate as I am, I only civilly desire to do
"the same, and it is denied to me!' A
"young bonze, who was standing by, and
"pleased with the resolution of the woman,
"told her, she was doing what was agree-
"able to her Deity, and that she would
"certainly be rewarded in the next world,
"by again meeting her husband, and being
"married to him anew. ' How !' cried
"she, ' meet my husband again, and be
"married anew to an old, jealous man!
"Burn yourself, if you please; I want no
"such rewards. I was in hopes to have
"made myself celebrated; but if that is all
"the recompence I am to have, I might as
"well stay where I am; and therefore, Mr.
"Governor, I beg leave to obey your com-
"mands."

I have the honour to be, &c.

LETTER

LETTER XXXV.

On the Laws of Scotland.

To C. C——r, Esq; the Temple, London.

Edinburgh, May 2, 1775.

SIR,

YOU desire me to send you some account of the Laws of this country: I should be very happy were it in my power to give you any information on this subject more adequate to your wishes. But without teazing you with apologies for what I cannot do, I will send you the best and shortest detail of them I can; and if I should not speak with all the precision such a topic may require, you will forgive me, I hope, when you remember, that all the little knowledge I have obtained, has been picked up at intervals, and by accident, in the course of a few months.

The Laws of Scotland have been collected to them from various places, and may be said to be the children of many fathers. They

They have their statutory or written Law, which comprehends the acts of parliament, made in the reign of James the First of Scotland; all those down to the Union with England; and, since the Union, all the acts which have passed the English Legislature in regard to Scotland. It comprehends likewise their acts of Sederunt, which are ordinances for regulating the forms of proceeding before the Court of Session, the Civil and the Canon Laws. Their unwritten or customary Law, is that which has gained its title by prescription, and been confirmed by subsequent decisions.

The penal Laws of Scotland are, in general, highly remarkable for their lenity, and as merciful as is consistent with the good of society. In cases of murder, the intention of the criminal, the *animus injuriandi* must be proved to infer the crime. In the old Laws of this country, there was a privilege reserved for that which was committed in sudden and inconsiderate acts of passion; but it was taken away afterwards, and homicide judged to be a capital crime without any such distinction. I know there are writers, and those sensible ones, who would, in no cafe, inflict the punifhment of death. They fay, that perpetual flavery would have a much greater effect in the eyes of every fociety, than the execution of a criminal: that a momentary terror is not the object we are to aim at, but a feries of remorfe and deteftation: that the contempt and indignation with which every one regards an executioner, is a proof in what light every one looks on the punifhment of death; and that it is abfurd, that thofe very Laws, which condemn and punifh homicide, fhould, in order to prevent murder, publicly commit murder themfelves. But without entering into a difquifition, whether fuch a punifhment is of benefit or not to the community, you will obferve, that the Scotch only act in obedience to that principle, which directs, at prefent, all other nations in this offence. The law of Mofes was the law of retaliation, and commanded, that he who had fpilt the blood of another, fhould lofe his own. Acts of mutilation and demembration are not punifhed with death in this Country. They have no " Black Act," as in England: the punifhment is the efcheat

of

of the possessions of the offender, which is far from being adequate to the crime.

The Laws of this country are equally severe with our own in regard to duelling. The man who kills his adversary in single combat, is punishable with death; but in all probability, a lenient interpretation would be given. The giver and receiver of a challenge, whether principal or second, is liable to be banished, and to have his possessions confiscated, even should no such combat take place. No similar case has occurred to my knowledge; but I imagine that the letter of this regulation would not be punctually complied with. Though there is no writing in the absolute defence of duels, I cannot but still think there are many and valid reasons for their being tolerated in every country. A thousand possible cases may occur, in which a man can have no redress, but by an appeal to the sword, and in which every other mode of terminating the dispute, would, in some measure, but aggravate the injury. In short, in all those cases which alone affect a man's honour, and of which his own feelings only

only can be the judge, the law of arms is the laſt and only reſource. On this point no preventive laws can ever take effect. A man of ſentiment only wiſhes to live ſo long as he can live with honour; nor can he ever balance betwixt the deſire of life, and becoming an object of contempt and deriſion. The only regulation that can ever be of ſervice in this reſpect, would be either making duels diſgraceful, or erecting a court of honour, to judge of the neceſſary reparation due to affronts.

The Laws againſt falſe impriſonment are nearly the ſame as with us. Every perſon who is wrongfully committed, has an act of damages againſt the judge or perſon who is guilty, from ſix hundred down to four hundred pounds Scots, according to his rank. Theſe damages are ſeldom modified by the Court of Seſſion; and with great propriety, as no greater and more real injuſtice can be done to ſociety, than robbing an innocent man of his liberty, detaining him in a loathſome priſon amongſt thoſe who are preſumed to be guilty, and affixing upon him a degree of infamy, which will not so easily pass away. The generality of the world, we know, never enquire whether a man is really culpable or not; they always conclude that he is so, from being in the circumstances of those that are culpable.

What is worthy of observation is, that there is no explicit statute in Scotland which punishes the commission of a rape with death. One would imagine, that the Scotch were great casuists on this point, and were fearful of drawing the line betwixt the unconsenting reluctance of Modesty, and the determined resistance of a tenacious and obstinate virtue, which is subdued only by force.

By the old Laws of Scotland, the punishment of theft was in proportion to the things stolen. This is increased gradually, and punishable with death, if the value of the theft amounts to thirty-two pennies Scotch, which, in the time of David the First, was the price of two sheep. In modern practice, however, the simple crime of stealing, unattended with any aggravating circumstances,

such

such as breaking into an house, or using violence, is punished by banishment, imprisonment, or the loss of effects; which is the method that reason would suggest. It is observable, that neither the Laws of Moses, nor those of Rome, punished theft capitally. The Marquis Beccaria, in his excellent Treatise on Crimes and Punishments, says, "That the punishment of robbery, not attended with violence, ought always to be pecuniary: that the man who endeavours to enrich himself with the property of another, should, in return, be deprived of part of his own: that in all cases, there should be a relation betwixt the crime and the punishment; but that betwixt the robbing of one person and the death of another, there is no similitude whatever."

It is an honour, in my opinion, to the Laws of Scotland, that in judging of this crime, they are so lenient; and the equitable consequences that flow from it, are a convincing proof, that it is as good in fact as in theory. The banishment of a citizen to other countries is a loss to his own; nor does he in the least benefit that society to which he is removed, by his example, because it is distant from the place where the crime was committed.

The aggravation of theft, which arises from the criminal having been before convicted of the same, and by which he becomes habit and repute a thief, is punishable, however, with death. The reason of this is just and obvious: the end of all punishment is to correct and to amend the offender; but here, it is visible, they have lost their effect. The man who has seen the evil consequences of such deeds, who has already experienced the lenity of the Laws, but who voluntarily and premeditatedly again offends society, by repeating his transgressions, can no longer be bound by the Laws; and therefore, unfit to be a member of society.

The crimes of piracy here are tried before the High Admiral, and punishable with death.

Forgery, if the deed has been put to use, is a capital offence. Where a person is found

found guilty of forgery by the Court of Seffion, he is by them remitted to the Jufticiary; an indictment is there exhibited againft him, and a jury fworn, before whom the decree already given by the Court of Seffion is held in place of all other evidence, and in refpect of which the offender is found guilty.

The punifhment of perjury, or fwearing falfely on an affize, is here punifhed by confifcation of moveables, imprifonment for a year, and infamy. Even all this, in my opinion, is too fmall. The man who endeavours to take away the life of another, by an oath falfely taken, ought, on conviction, to lofe his own. Great allowance fhould certainly be made by every Judge for inadvertency, forgetfulnefs, &c. but when wilful and direct perjury is evident on the very face of the depofition; when he depofes in one part to what he contradicts in another; in fhort, when his whole vifible intention is to deprive another man of his property or his life, the fentence of retaliation is the fmalleft that ought to take place againft him. The fame difpofition which would

lead

lead a witness, in a cool and dispassionate manner, in the eye of the Public, in the solemnity of a court of justice, in total disregard of truth, to swear away the life of a fellow-creature, would induce him to take it away by any other means, if he had the chance to escape.

I have now, I think, given you all the leading outlines of those more atrocious offences, which, by the Scotch Law, extend their consequences to life, exile, imprisonment, or heavy pecuniary fines. You will observe great clemency in the letter; and I can assure you, from some little knowledge of my own, and from better information, there is equal mildness observed in the interpreting of them. Independent of these, there are other institutions which do the Scotch equal honour. No person can be imprisoned in order for trial, without a warrant in writing expressing the cause, and proceeding upon a subscribed information. Every prisoner in this country, committed to trial, if the crime be not a capital one, of which he is accused, is entitled to be released on giving bail. I do not mention these

these circumstances as confined to this country alone; I mention them as marks of liberty, justice, and sound reason. Every man who is tried here, on a prosecution of an higher nature, is tried before a jury of fifteen men, chosen and agreed to by himself, out of a body of forty-five. On this trial, it is not necessary, by the Laws of Scotland, that the jury should be unanimous in their verdict, either in condemning or acquitting the accused: the smallest possible majority either way is sufficient. The wrong and perverted judgment of one individual can alone affect his own single voice; the rest are left at liberty to vote according to their consciences. The juries in Scotland have now an uncontroverted right to give what verdict they think proper: By the old Laws, they had not a liberty to acquit a prisoner when there was a clear proof of his guilt. A remarkable case of this kind once happened, in which a jury of the prisoner's peers pronounced him innocent, when there was the most undoubted evidence of his being guilty. A jury of twenty-five Gentlemen of landed property were called

upon

upon to try this writ of error in affize, and the former jury were punifhed by imprifonment for a year, forfeiture of moveables, and infamy. The mode is now abolifhed.

The execution of fentence paffed on a criminal is now limited to eight days on the fouth fide of the river Forth, and twelve days on the north fide of it, by an act of the third of George the Second. Formerly the term was of much longer continuance, and a criminal was fuffered to remain fometimes forty days in the horrors of darknefs, uncertain of his fate, and executed at laft. It is in reality the higheft act of clemency as well as juftice, that fentences fhould be executed immediately; that they fhould appear in the eyes of the common people what they really are, the confequence of the crime, and that the ideas of crime and punifhment fhould be affociated as much as poffible.

I have not determined upon what apology I can make for fending fo much Law to a Lawyer without a fee. I know, however, you are a patriot, and that you will be happy to fee a code of Laws fo favourable to the liberty of mankind, in a country which has been
celebrated

celebrated for sentiments of a very different nature. With what justice they have been blamed, I leave you to determine, and how far you are to trust those who make a trade of scandal, and live by defamation. Should you not inform me in your next letter, that you are already sick of the subject, I shall take the liberty to continue these remarks.

I have the honour to be, &c.

LETTER XXXVI.

The Commissary Court, and other inferior Courts.

To C. C—r, Esq. the Temple, London.

Edinburgh, May 5, 1775.

SIR,

AFTER having made you acquainted with some of the Laws of Scotland, it is but proper that I should now introduce you to some of the courts where those laws are dispensed: "Where the poor and the father-"less are taken compassion on, and where "those are helped to right who suffer wrong." Let us visit, if you please, the Commissary Court, which is situated in a place called the Parliament Close, and which, though it has not the most promising appearance, is still a Court of some business and great importance. It is a little room of about ten feet square, and, from the darkness and dirtiness of it, you would rather imagine that those who were brought into it, were confined there. To this Chamber of Justice you ascend by a narrow, dismal, wind-
ing

ing ſtair-caſe, and where you are in danger of falling every ſtep you take. During the reign of Popery, and the infallibility of the Pope, this Court was ſtyled *Curia Chriſtianitatis*; but alas! times are much altered both with the Pope and the Court; and ſince the Head has been found to be very fallible, ſome people ſeem to think, that the Members are not leſs ſo.

At preſent this Court acknowledges the King as its Lord; and he appoints the four Judges who preſide there. Their powers are ſtill very extenſive, and their abilities very great: though, to ſpeak the truth, they have occaſion for them all; for, as Scrubb ſays, " They have a power of buſineſs upon their " hands." All thoſe ladies who want huſbands, and who can no longer do without them, ſet forth their neceſſities in the prettieſt manner poſſible, and are relieved. All thoſe ladies too, who are tired of the huſbands they have already got, and are very deſirous of getting quit of them in a decent manner, mention their wants, and are relieved likewiſe.—Nothing can come amiſs to ſo much Juſtice.—The Commiſſaries know the wants

of

of the ladies, and satisfy them all in the most obliging manner.

Sometimes a very amiable and modest lady comes to make her complaint in regard to the impotence of her husband; and favours them (for they love precision) with an agreeable detail of what he cannot do. They immediately take compassion on so much virtue and delicacy, and give her an opportunity of meeting with better fortune another time. In short, I can hardly enumerate the cases they treat successfully: it is said they perform more Cures than the whole College of Physicians, and are particularly famous for giving ease in desperate complaints.

But it is not to these instances alone their attention is confined: — they fulfill and interpret the last wills and testaments of the Dead. The desires of the Living are easily known and satisfied; but the intentions of those who are gone are not soon discovered: but that is nothing; for the Commissaries know every thing.

In all the trials which come before this Court, the evidences there given, are taken down in writing, which is not only very tedious,

dious, but unneceffary; for, properly, every Court ought to hear the witneffes themfelves. Every witnefs does not literally fpeak the truth, but his countenance always does. It often happens, indeed too often, that a man's looks give the lie to every thing he fays, and that you read in his face the defigned purpofe of deceiving you. How is this to be carrried down upon paper? Who is to mark this to other Judicatures before whom it may appear? Who fhall draw the exact line betwixt the doubtful timidity, the bafhful hefitation of a modeft man who fpeaks the truth, and the unconcerned impudence of a fellow who difregards every thing and every body, and who has got his evidence by heart? You frequently find, that the moft plaufible evidence upon paper, is that which you would leaft have trufted from the witnefs's own mouth. The teftimony, likewife, in this Court, is given by Interrogatories; which is certainly the worft method that could be devifed for finding out the truth—as they frequently fuggeft to a witnefs what he is to fay. The Law very juftly forbids all interrogations which directly tend to condemn a man's felf; according

ing to its own Maxim, "*Nemo tenetur jurare* "*in suam turpitudinem* ;" and yet authorises an immediate question which suggests the condemnation of another, and which, in all human probability, had the witness been left to tell the fact in his own terms, he never meant to say.

The Oath that is here administered to a witness is reckoned peculiarly solemn; and those who entertain very favourable opinions of human nature, think it so solemn that it is impossible that any one should break it.— That you may judge of that matter I send it to you. The evidence is ordered to kneel down, to lay his right hand upon the bible, and to repeat these words after the Judge:

" I renounce all the blessings contained in
" this holy book, if I do not tell the truth:
" I wish all the curses therein contained may
" be my portion, if I do not tell the truth:
" and I swear by the Almighty God himself,
" as I shall answer to Him at the great day
" of judgment, that I will tell the truth, the
" whole truth, and nothing but the truth."

All this, I will grant you, is very solemn, and what no person of any feeling would think
of

of violating—but over a villain all ties are insufficient.

But what is the moſt extraordinary of all is, that they do not bring out this great Oath in all caſes; but have, what they call, *a little Oath*, to ſerve common occaſions. My God, Sir, *a little Oath!* What a proſtitution of terms! As if, in the eye of a man of feeling and underſtanding, all oaths were not equally binding. Can ſuch legiſlators wonder that very little attention ſhould be paid even to the greateſt oath? Indeed I much fear that a very trifling degree of confidence is to be placed in a man, who is called upon to give his teſtimony in a cauſe where his own intereſt is deeply concerned. Monteſquieu ſays, " *C'eſt toujours par un retour ſur eux-mêmes que* " *les hommes agiſſent: nul n'eſt mauvais-grâ-* " *tuitement: il faut qu'il y ait une raiſon qui* " *determine; et cette raiſon eſt toujours une* " *raiſon d'intérêt.*" If this be true, which I am afraid it is, very little regard is ever to be paid to any evidence when not corroborated by circumſtances; and indeed the greateſt judges have never paid any. Circumſtances and probability are the only foundations on which

any

any reliance is to be placed. Evidences have been bought and sold: the worst will swear according to orders; and even the best mistake meanings, and give interpretations of their own. But circumstances can never deceive; and every man is a judge how far such an act is probable.

The gentlemen who officiate in the Commissary Court are styled Proctors, and are in general very ignorant of every thing but their business. The Advocates do not plead in this Court; they sometimes give in Memorials like the *Procurateurs* in the French courts; and it is on the ingenuity of these that the cause frequently turns. These Memorials are intended, it is said, to " elucidate justice;"— by which is meant, each party makes it out in his own favour.

But what will surprise you most in this Court is, that the Judges are paid their salaries from the causes which come under their hands. You may imagine that such a thing is impossible; but I assure you it is a fact; and though nothing can be more improper,

nothing

nothing is more true. I am naturally inclined to think every man honeſt: I would imagine they acted from a principle incapable of being corrupted; but I am very ſorry to think that there is ſuch an opening for injuſtice on the one hand, and for injurious ſuſpicions on the other. When a Judge affixes ſuch a particular ſum of money for ſuch a particular ſentence, moderated, as he ſuppoſes, to the abilities of the party, how liable is he to be deceived? or rather, how is it poſſible that he can be otherwiſe? how diſhonourable is it that Juſtice ſhould be purchaſed? and how much more diſgraceful, that one man ſhould buy it at one price, and another man at another? If it is to be brought to market, there ſhould be one fixed market-price, and every man ought to pay the ſame for it as his neighbours.

You will remember with me how much that act, which made the Judges ſalaries independent of the Crown, was admired in England; tho' the intereſts of Government could not often interfere with thoſe of individuals, and

and consequently but remotely to be dreaded. But what alterations will you think necessary here, when a Judge has it in his power to set what value he pleases on the decrees which his office and a common regard to justice oblige him to give: when he is permitted to say, " Thus much shalt thou pay me; I decreed " in thy favour, and I demand it."

In the most disinterested hands such a power is always liable to suspicion. When there arises a contest betwixt a remote and doubtful principle of Equity, and an immediate and certain one of Advantage; when the pronouncing one kind of sentence produces such a sum of money, and another such a sum; what a fund of innate honour must that man possess, who invariably and constantly determines according to what is just and right, without any regard to emoluments of his own! But should this licence ever fall into dishonest men's hands, and such a case may happen, I should tremble, not only for the sake of those unfortunate people who might chance to come under their decisions, but for the very being of Justice herself. Many of them, I imagine,

I imagine, would cry out with the poor Peasant in the French Comedy, "Alas! I have "gained my Process, and have lost all my "Money."

There still remain three other inferior Courts, which I will mention to you before I conclude this letter.

The first is that of the Bailies'; which is likewise situated in the Parliament-close. It sits in the forenoon three days in every week; where one of the Bailies of the Town (who answer to our Common Councilmen) presides. He is informed and assisted in his office by one of the City Assessors, who is to be an Advocate. In this Court both civil and criminal cases are tried; but the criminal ones are not to be of a capital nature, or infer death.

Another is styled the Dean of Gild's Court; who is a Magistrate of the Borough, and has cognizance of the mercantile causes in the Borough.

The third is the Sheriff's Court; and is intended for the convenience of the Poor, and the recovery of Small Debts. Ten marks is the
highest

higheſt ſum that can be ſued for in it, except in the caſe of ſervants wages, which are not limited. An old writer ſays, "Thate for the "caſe of ſaide Poore the expence of a pro- "ceſſe amounteth onlie to ſex-pence." This is a pleaſant kind of a Court, and might furniſh a good example to all its neighbours. But the Law, which is a nice obſerver of forms, and hates innovations of all ſorts, will neither receive good counſel, nor profit by good example. Law and Phyſic, from the extravagance of the charges in each, were once the ſubject of frequent compariſons; but the parallel will hold no longer. A man who cannot afford to be regularly well, ſteps out of the preſcribed road, and applies to a Quack, where, by taking a bottle of the "Reſtorative Electuary," or the "Elixir of "Life," he either gets well, or is put out of the power of making complaints. But the man who is aggrieved "in the means where- "by he lives," finds no perſon ready to do his buſineſs for a little money; and though he may begin *ſub forma Pauperis*, he always finiſhes in that condition. In this profeſſion there

there are no Quacks who advertise " No Cure " no Pay," and who tell you, as they do in medicine, " if your case is bad, never mind: " if you are a dying, so much the better— " come to me, I shall cure you."

I have the honour to be, &c.

LETTER XXXVII.

The Supreme Courts of Edinburgh.

To C. C——r, Esq. the Temple, London.

Edinburgh, May 7, 1775.

SIR,

IN my last letter, I mentioned to you the inferior Courts which are held in this City; in compliance with your request, I now send you some little account of what are styled here the Supreme ones. I have only your own desires to plead against the dulness of such a subject.

The Judge who is appointed to try all the maritime causes, civil as well as criminal, is named the High Admiral. His jurisdiction extends likewise to all such as fall within flood-mark, the harbours, and the creeks. In these cases, his power is sole and absolute, nor subject to a review of the Court of Session, except by reduction or suspension: but they can carry no cause against him.

The Court of Exchequer exercises its jurisdiction in all questions of the revenue. It consists, properly speaking, of the Lord High Treasurer of Great Britain, a Chief Baron, with four other Barons of Exchequer. These Barons, to obtain their title, must be serjeants at law, English barristers, or Scotch advocates of five years standing. The Barons enjoy all the privileges which belong to the Lords of Session. This Court extends its jurisdiction to the duties of the customs and excise. It is said, I know not with what truth, that there is more villainy and perjury to be met with in this Court than in any other in Scotland; which is, I assure you, saying a great deal.

The Supreme criminal Judge in this kingdom was anciently styled the Justiciar. He held two courts every year at Edinburgh, where all the freeholders of the kingdom were assembled; but this, as you may easily suppose, from the inconvenience of the custom, went out of practice. Eight deputies were then appointed, from which number every quarter of the kingdom had two assigned them as Judges, who were to make

make their circuits in April and October. This mode was afterwards changed; and five of the Lords of Seffion were added under the title of Lords Commiffioners of Juftidiary, to the Juftice General. Two of thefe Judges are appointed to hold Circuits in certain boroughs of each diftrict, into which they go twice a year. In cafe of illnefs or other accidents, one Judge may proceed to bufinefs, without the affiftance of his brother.

The laft Court, with which I fhall clofe this long account, is that of the Lords of Seffion, which is the Supreme one in this country, and to which all others appeal. It is not only confidered as competent to points of Law, but of Equity, and may be faid to unite in itfelf the two powers of the Court of King's Bench and the Court of Chancery. The decifions which are given here are univerfally refpected in this country, and I believe with juftice. They are fubject, however, to be reviewed by the Englifh Houfe of Peers, to whom the privileges of the Scotch parliament were conveyed. In fome inftances, the decrees of
thefe

these Supreme Courts have been different: the moſt remarkable one was that of the Douglas cauſe, in which the deciſions were directly oppoſite. I leave it to themſelves to reconcile theſe different ideas of juſtice; the Scotch, however, in general, ſtill retain their opinions.

The Court of Seſſion took its name from being appointed to hold a certain number of ſeſſions in one place, inſtead of being unfixed and itinerant as it was formerly. In its origin, it conſiſted of ſeven laymen and ſeven churchmen, with a preſident, who was generally a prelate; but when churchmen were diſqualified from temporal juriſdiction, they loſt their ſeats, and have never ſince reſumed them.

The Judges of this Court, who cannot become ſuch till after twenty-five years of age, have always been received by warrant from the King. It is likewiſe a neceſſary qualification, that they ſhould have ſerved as an advocate or principal clerk of ſeſſion for five years, or as a writer for ten years. When any vacancy happens, the King preſents the ſucceſſor by a letter addreſſed to the Lords,

Lords, wherein they are required to try and admit the person named. Their present number is fifteen, and the decisions are carried by a majority.

The College of Justice, as the Court of Session is styled, comprehends not only the Judges but the Advocates who plead before them, the Clerks of Session, and the Writers to the Signet. The privileges which are annexed to the College, extend equally to all the members. They are exempted from paying the minister's stipend, and all customs, &c. imposed upon goods carried to or from the City of Edinburgh.

Their own proper civil jurisdiction in the first instance is very extensive, and in which they judge exclusive of all inferior Courts whatever. In the second, they judge only by review; but the causes here are many, as there lies from almost every Court, and in almost every case, a right of appeal.

The Gentlemen who are styled Advocates in this country, are almost innumerable; for every man who has nothing to do, and no better name to give himself, is called Advocate. Of those, however, who practise
and

and get business, the number is extremely few; but amongst these few, are some men whose abilities are not only an honour to the profession, but to the country itself: Men who make the bar a school of eloquence, and not, as I am sorry to say with us, a jargon of barbarous and almost unintelligible words, and who preserve, in their debates, the manners and sentiments of Gentlemen. I know, that though a lawyer, you have lamented, as well as every other man, that species of illiberal invective, that total disregard of decency and almost of truth, that entire want of all the spirit which a genteel education generally bestows, so remarkable in our own Council. A young practitioner at our bar, often imagines, that it is impossible to be impudent enough; and that impertinence, far from being a sign of ignorance, is a mark of abilities. Without mentioning the inhumanity of abusing those people who neither are allowed, nor can have it in their power to defend themselves; I own, for my part, I see no more right that a Counsel at the bar has to insult you with affronts, than a Clergyman would have

to

to address you from the pulpit, or an officer on a review day to knock you down: but if, like some other quarrelsome animals in England, it should be found necessary to suffer them to fight, in order to keep up their courage, let lawyer attack lawyer, till after having snarled, and bit, and torn each other, till they are weary, they may fall to picking up what they can get, in peace and good fellowship.

I have the honour to be, &c.

LETTER

LETTER XXXVIII.

On the Scotch Laws relative to Marriage.

To C. C———r, Esq; the Temple, London.

Edinburgh, May 10, 1775.

SIR,

IN most countries, the ceremonies of Marriage are treated with respect. A Roman Catholic considers them as one of the duties of his religion; and even an Englishman looks upon the solemnization of it as a serious thing; but here, it is matter of merriment, and no ceremony at all is necessary. A man, indeed, in Scotland, can scarce be said to know whether he is married or not, as his own consent is no part of the business. It is sufficient that two or three people determine it without his participation. A woman who has no money nor much virtue, takes it into her head that it would be a very proper thing for her to marry such a man, and she does it. She brings two people to swear, that he called her his wife, and

and that they paſſed the night together as ſuch. There is not the leaſt occaſion that there ſhould be one word of truth in all this, or that people who are unconcerned ſhould believe it; but notwithſtanding that, a Marriage is confirmed according to Law, wiſely made for that purpoſe. In vain the poor man would ſay that he did not know the woman; that if he had, he ſhould never have thought of marrying her, or even bring creditable witneſſes to the truth of what he ſays; nobody doubts it, but he is married for all that, and every body laughs at him. It is poſſible, indeed, that in ſuch a caſe, a woman would make the moſt of what ſhe could get, and take a ſum of money from one, that ſhe may have an opportunity of impoſing upon another: for though, unfortunately, ſhe can but marry one huſband at a time, ſhe may attempt to marry a thouſand. No traffic can be more profitable, while it has the ſanction of the Laws, than this is. It is enriching a very amiable part of the ſex in a very laudable manner, and opening an extenſive field, in which women of genius may ſhew their abilities.

A Clergy-

A Clergyman of a large parish in England, when his parishioners are matrimonially inclined, is the only person who may be said to enjoy the benefits of Matrimony: but were he in this country, though he might be very willing, nobody would give him an opportunity of exercising his function, or receiving the profits of it. Here is no occasion for any particular ceremony; two people have only to agree to call themselves Man and Wife, and they are so. By the Roman Law the consent of the father was necessary to the marriage of the child; but it was found to be very absurd that a child could not act as he thought proper; and so it is ordained by the Laws of Scotland, that the children may marry as soon as they please, and the parents, if they do not approve of it, may rail by themselves.

The Judges, however, who sometimes have these points under their consideration, seem ashamed of the extravagance and absurdity of their own laws; and when there is any equitable possibility, always determine against them. Indeed, to say the truth, such laws as these are a scandal to society, and teeming

with all the evil consequences bad institutions generally produce. Every one knows that clandestine marriages were put a stop to in England from the many impositions that were practised; and that even the multiplication of society was by no means adequate to the misfortunes it sustained from them. But in those cases a ceremony was performed by a regular Clergyman in priest's orders, with the consent of both parties. There was a formal and legal act solemnized in the presence of witnesses, before whom they mutually agreed, and did actually become man and wife. In Scotland, however, the case is entirely different: the law says in one instance, " that a
" marriage is fully perfected by Consent,
" which, without any consummation, founds
" all the conjugal rights and duties."—In another instance, " that a consummation after
" a promise of marriage forms an actual mar-
" riage."—And in a third instance, " that
" it is not necessary that the marriage
" should be celebrated by a Clergyman, but
" that the consent of the parties may be de-
" clared before any witnesses whatever."

You here observe that the character of the witness is not the least necessary; and therefore there is no occasion to be difficult in the choice of one, as any will be sufficient. But this is not all.—These beneficent and gallant Legislators, who take such care of young women, and provide what is proper for them, further say, " that even should no formal " consent appear, Marriage is presumed from " cohabitation." In England a poor fellow runs his neck into the noose wilfully, and with his eyes open: but in Scotland, here are so many snares and toils, and gins and pitfalls, that a man must be endued with uncommon dexterity, not to be entrapped by some of them.

In reading some cases of this kind this morning, the uncommon hardship of one particularly struck me.—A woman proved with child by a man, who, on a visit to her at her lying-in, and probably in tenderness to her at such a moment, called her his Wife in the presence of the Midwife—And on no better foundation, without any antecedent circumstance proved, without having cohabited together,

gether, without either habite or repute, were thefe two people, by a folemn decifion of the laws of Scotland, adjudged to be Man and Wife. And now what think you of thefe Laws? You will imagine, I fuppofe, from hence, that there is nobody of a certain age unmarried. But, as I have already told you, though many attempts are made to infer fuch kind of nuptials, they are conftantly almoft difcouraged by the Judges. And indeed were it not for that *vis inertiæ* which may be faid to refide in Them, I know not what could refift the deftructive force of thefe regulations. You will agree with me in thinking them ftill more fatal, when you recollect that this place is the feat of an univerfity to which fome hundreds of young men annually refort; many of them of the moft refpectable families; all of them at a time of life when they are but too fufceptible of the tender impreffions, and but too eafily impofed upon by any woman who has art enough to make herfelf appear an object of affection: many of them ignorant of the laws in this refpect, and liable, from the unguarded inexperience of youth, to be drawn into expreffions which can never be be recalled. When the Scotch weigh thefe circumftances, when they confider the reputation of their Univerfity, and how much it is their duty to guard againft thefe impofitions, it becomes matter of lefs wonder that fuch marriages never take effect; for there are very few inftances of their being confirmed. The firft thing the Scotch in general do to ftrangers, is to put them on their guard againft thefe practices.

Notwithftanding this fpirit of Matrimony, there never was a place where fo many women of loofe character were to be met with at every corner. It may indeed feem the neceffary progrefs, that the woman who voluntarily has recourfe to law for an hufband fhould, in fome moment, have admitted certain perfons to the privilege of one, without any law at all. It is highly requifite, therefore, that the line betwixt a fingle and a married ftate fhould be ftrongly marked; for when no ceremony is neceffary in the change from one ftate to the other, a woman is too apt to make no ceremony of the matter.

In fpite of the facility of their marriages, the Scotch feem inclined to a fingle life, and many

many months pass away without a marriage taking place. While the English are constantly flying down hither to get married, the people here look on with great indifference, and wonder how they can travel four hundred miles for so foolish a purpose. The employment of a Clergyman, I am told, on the borders, is very lucrative; for, as the English are generally in a great hurry to be married, as well as for every other thing, he proportions his demands to their impatience. Were our countrymen and their brides who make these expeditions, a little more acquainted with the laws of this Country, they might set at defiance " the benefit of the Clergy," as " the laws which Love has made" are sufficiently binding.

I have the honour to be, &c.

LETTER XXXIX.

Some Peculiarities in the Scotch Laws.

To C. C—r, Esq. the Temple, London.

Edinburgh, May 12, 1775.

SIR,

THERE are some particularities in the Laws of Scotland, which are not only a contradiction to the principles of all Laws whatever, but a disgrace even to common sense. It is generally an allowed maxim, ' that no question can be put to a man, which ' has an immediate tendency to condemn him- ' self;' and yet, in contradiction to this very maxim which they have adopted, there is in some points a reference had to the party's own oath to condemn or acquit himself. This is styled the " Oath of Probation," and is used in those cases when the other party has not proof sufficient to establish what he wishes. By all laws, and in all cases whatever, every man should be presumed innocent till he is proved to be guilty. In matters of right there

is

is no such thing as a demi-proof; it is either entirely established, or not established at all, unless one can suppose there is such a thing as demi-truth. But notwithstanding this, when a certain degree of probability is inferred, the Judge orders the party to swear, whether or no what his adversary alleges be true; and by that means either to condemn himself, or gain his point, by his own oath, in direct contradiction to another law of their own, which says, ' that no man can establish a right ' by his own oath.'

If you add to this, the little credit that will be given to any man who is acquitted by such means, the temptation it offers for perjury, and the very easy opportunity it gives to every man who really may be guilty, of clearing himself with an appearance of honour, you will, I am sure, agree with me in thinking that nothing could be more absurd. An appeal to oath, like the antient appeals to single combat, confounds the innocent with the criminal, and gives an equal power to them both.

Another peculiarity in the Scotch Laws, which

which you will think equally improper, is the Judicial Examination. The party who bring the action being able to prove nothing, beg leave of the Court to examine the defendant in the way they think beſt, by aſking him what queſtions they chooſe, and which tend to make the interrogated either contradict himſelf, or utter what they wiſh him to ſay. This mode of examination is that which the Inquiſition adopts, as beſt ſuited to its purpoſes, where they find the poor ſufferer guilty in ſpite of all he can ſay to the contrary. In England, whenever an accuſed perſon is permitted to ſpeak, it is held to be in his own defence. On the contrary, by theſe laws he is obliged to ſpeak, and what he does ſay is only calculated to condemn himſelf. In theſe caſes the Judges make uſe of a kind of judicial arithmetic, and multiply and ſubtract at their pleaſure; for what the defendant ſays in his own favour, they very naturally conclude is partiality to himſelf, and overlook it accordingly: but ſhould he ſay any thing againſt himſelf, they as naturally imagine that he would ſay as little as he poſſibly could, that he might probably

probably conceal half the truth, and therefore they set it right by believing just double of what is the fact.

A third mode of proceeding, equally as unjust as the other two, is when a party wishes to remove any witnesses he thinks may be against him in a cause, and who might be a means of his losing it. In such a situation he begs leave to object Partial Counsel; by which is understood, their having mentioned the subject to any indifferent third person, who, probably, has no knowledge of the cause. The character or reputation of the person is nothing to the purpose: he is found guilty of speaking, and is condemned accordingly. In the proper management of these circumstances lies the whole strength of the cause: and a man frequently gains his point, not by the facts he establishes, and the witnesses he brings, but by the witnesses he removes, and the truth which he conceals. A poor man who fancies he is sure of victory by the testimonies which he has to-day, may find, to-morrow, that he may as well have had none, as they are all taken from him.

But if this artifice should fail, there is still
another

another to fucceed it: they beg leave to affure the Judge the witneffes have no character. A woman, for inftance, they allege has had knowledge of man improperly, and therefore cannot fpeak the truth. They attribute to the tafting this forbidden fruit the reverfe of what our Firft Mother experienced; and inftead of teaching them " the knowledge " of good and evil," they pronounce they do not know one from the other. In vain, Sir, a man of plain underftanding would fay, that this circumftance has no relation to fpeaking the truth, or that having purfued their own inclinations in one point, can in no meafure prevent them from following the dictates of their confcience in another, where they can have no inclination to miflead them. You might as well talk to the " deaf Adder;" for thefe humane laws, which are fo favourable to the women in fome inftances, lay it down as a principle in this point, ' that after the com-
' miffion of certain freedoms, there is no truth
' in woman.'

Though fuch particulars as thefe are a difgrace to all laws, and the bane of every fociety, yet we meet with them in every place, and
they

they are suffered to remain without alteration. How strange is it, that every political institution should be distinguished by something that is absurd and ridiculous, and that wherever we turn our eyes we should discover only a confused scene of contradictions, uncertainty, hardships, and arbitrary power! What more mortifying picture can we have of human weakness! As if every thing which is the work of man must be marked with imbecillity, and those very laws which punish injustice in others, should be disgraced by injustice of our own.

I have the honour to be, &c.

LETTER

LETTER XL.

A View from Rosline Castle.

To R. D. Esq.

Edinburgh, May 15, 1775.

SIR,

WERE any man of my acquaintance desirous of seeing the sublime and beautiful in perfection, according to Mr. Burke's definition of them, I would bring him into Scotland. For the beautiful, for the softer, and more finished charms, I would shew him the Ladies, who are, in my humble opinion, the most beautiful objects in the creation. For the sublime, I would deliver him to all the naked wildness and extended desolation of the country.

The style of an English landscape is that of improved and cultivated nature. Though frequently highly romantic, it is in general too diminutive, and its prospect too confined. The

The eye with great ease comprehends the whole of it at one view: but in this country, there is a certain character of greatness and majesty observable in every part. Nature seems to act at large; all her works are bold, strong, and unfettered by the improvements of art.

Added to this, the appearance of the heavens is not less uncommon than the face of the country, or less diversified. The winds, which here reign with peculiar violence, allow none of that placid and serene sky which gives an air of tranquillity and chearfulness to every scene. The clouds, driven on by the impetuosity of the storms, assume a thousand fantastic shapes, and changing as suddenly, put on others equally as strange. Nor am I surprised at the wild imagination of Ossian, " bodying them forth" into beings of his own creation; into the souls of departed heroes, or wicked spirits big with death and desolation.

Not many days ago, I beheld one of the most picturesque scenes the imagination can possibly paint. It was Rosline Castle, near Edinburgh.

The day was uncommonly fine for this season of the year, and gave me every advantage I could desire.

On my left hand lay the Castle of Rosline, now in ruins. The arched gateway which led to it, and on which the sun shone very bright, shewed every mark which time and the inclemency of the seasons that had passed over it, had made in its walls. Within the gate stood the mouldering remains of the Castle itself, disposed in broken and shapeless columns, scattered here and there; some rising in the air to a great height, others level with the ground, some covered over with ivy, others left bare and naked, but all of them bearing the venerable marks of its former grandeur and magnificence. The sun, which now darted its rays amidst the broken arches, and then again was overshadowed by the clouds, shewed them to still greater advantage. Above the Castle, on the left side, rose a steep hill, the side of which was beautifully covered with wood up to the very top, except where the bare rock now and then made its appearance, or a sheet of water
rushed

ruſhed down in precipitate falls to the bottom.

On the hill where I ſtood, which was without the Caſtle, lay in a ſtrange kind of diſorder, the fragments of what had formerly been the out-buildings of the Caſtle. At preſent nothing remained in any diſcoverable form, but the arch of a window, through which was a beautiful perſpective of the country below you. Nothing could be a ſtronger picture of ruin than this arch. Its ſtones were mouldering in decay, its figure had already began to be loſt, and part of it now fallen. An old tree, which grew by it, had thruſt its withered branches through the wall, and waving with the blaſt, cauſed an hollow and mournful ſound, which, had it been in the dead of night, in ſilence, and darkneſs, might have intimidated the moſt courageous.

Below the place where I ſtood, lay a ſmall plain ſurrounded with hills, which gradually roſe above it. A little, but neat farm houſe added beauty to this ſpot. It was disjoined from the land on which the Caſtle was ſituated,

ated, by a rivulet of water. The whole scene was a picture of quiet and retirement. It was sheltered on every side; no storms could incommode it; and should its inhabitant have ever have known a desire to wander, he had only to look upwards to the Castle of Rosline, to see the nothingness of all human grandeur; the pride and strength of ages mouldering into dust.

The hills, which immediately surrounded this plain, were covered with the finest verdure: the sheep that were feeding on them, and the sun shining over their surface, gave them the most lively and picturesque air imaginable. Beyond these rose another chain of hills, entirely buried in snow, and which, though probably at many miles distance, appeared in the prospect close upon them. Paint to yourself the extreme beauty of this contrast. The one in all the luxuriancy of vegetation, of the most lively green, the next cloathed in all the horrors of winter! It was the union of two seasons, as opposite in reality, as they now seemed joined in appearance. Above these last hills, as if to close

the

the scene, appeared the Highlands, in all the aweful majesty of superior height and grandeur.

I am afraid that I describe these beauties to you but very imperfectly; for no words can be adequate to the grandeur of such a subject. As I had nothing to note them with at the time, the strength and vivacity of the first impression is somewhat worn away. But I was rather willing to hazard your censures in this instance, than neglect giving you some faint notion of the scenes of this Country.

I have the honour to be, &c.

LETTER XLI.

On the Dancing Masters Balls, and Publics.

To Miss Lucinda B——

Edinburgh, May 15, 1775.

MY last letter, I am afraid, afforded my dear Lucinda little worth her acceptance. The defect of matter of greater importance in this Country, which is all Quiet and Serenity, and, like the upper regions, has no share in the storms of that below, must plead my excuse for this epistle; unless you will agree with me, in the words of Sir William Temple on the like occasion, " that as " men have more curiosity to enquire how a " great man sleeps, than what a mean man " *does* all the day long;" so the very rest and idleness of this northern people, seems more worth knowing than the busy motions of many small ones on the other side the Atlantic, who yet at this time pretend to be considered, and make a noise.

I think I have told you every thing relating

lating to the public assemblies: but there are others which seem to afford the Scotch great entertainment, as they are much frequented, and in general more crowded than the others. These are Dancing-masters Balls, who swarm in Edinburgh, and who are constantly exhibiting their scholars to the public. You know 'tis a custom in London for some of the principal Dancing-masters to have balls for their benefit; but here it is a general thing, from the one most in vogue, to the humble teacher of a reel to the drone of the bagpipe. Each has his ball and his public, or his two balls (for I can find no difference) at a particular season of the year, in the Assembly-room; where a degree of emulation fires their breast, and each endeavours to shew his own excellence and skill as a master, by the execution and performance of his scholars. It is incredible the pleasure and satisfaction the inhabitants of this City take in this diversion. They seem to enjoy it much more than dancing themselves: I suppose from the pleasing remembrance of those happy times when they themselves made part of the entertainment. But on other accounts I cannot wonder at it:

as it is not only an entertaining fight, but fills the mind with agreeable reflections, and benevolence, to behold the rising generation in any part of their education that may hereafter contribute either to their own pleasure, or the advantage of society and mankind. I could not but admire the young ambition just glimmering forth in a Minuet or Country-dance, which, when roused into a flame, might hereafter aspire to a peerage and coronet: and that self-same grace and elegance dawning in a Bow, which might be destined to persuade a multitude, or command a senate. But besides the satisfaction arising to a thoughtful mind, from the consideration of so many of the human species being rendered completely happy, in the full meridian of innocent youth, without any pain, any anxious care, any world in the opposite scale to counterbalance the least portion of their enjoyment; I assure you, 'tis no despicable amusement, even as a puppet-shew, to behold so many beautiful little figures displaying their agility and graceful attitudes, as it were in a moving concert.

The children on these occasions are dressed
with

with much elegance, ease, and propriety; without the foppery of the French, or negligence of the English. You neither see a Boy of ten years old in the habillement of a *petit maître*, with bag, solitaire, sword, and muff: or the Youth of seventeen with his hair dishevelled, in the dress of an infant. The Scotch gain great credit by the apparel of their children, especially the young ones, who indeed are fine subjects for the display of taste in this particular.

I do not suppose any nation in Europe is more beautiful than the Scotch for a certain time; but the shape and symmetry of the boys, the complexion and features of the female sex, continue but a short period; as men, they are too coarse and ill-fashioned to be handsome; as women, too masculine and robust to be beauties. They dress their children in fancy-dresses, rather than any regular one; particularly the heads of the girls, which they ornament in the most unaffected pleasing manner possible, with ribbands and flowers: the habit of the boys also is elegant and plain: the performers, therefore, as to outside appearance,

pearance, have every thing to recommend and set off their excellence in dancing.

But I cannot say, they are any great proficients in any style of dancing that requires grace: the Scotch are perfect strangers to it in any part of their life. Agility and strength are most natural to them, are their darling delight, which they endeavour to improve from their earliest infancy, and in which they arrive at much perfection. But as many people take the greatest pains to accomplish what they will never obtain; so the inhabitants of this country exhaust much time in learning a minuet, the most requisite part of which they never arrive at, namely, that elegant and graceful air which is the very essence of it, and of which the Italians and French are the only complete masters.

But if the Scotch are deprived of this advantage to their persons, all-provident Nature has bestowed on them others, which are of much greater use to themselves and society. The want of grace is abundantly recompensed by a superiority of strength and manliness, and that sinewy arm, the very sight of which

is

is sufficient to make a pampered offspring of the south stand amazed and tremble.

At these balls all the children dance minuets; which would be very tiresome and disagreeable, as well from the badness of the performance, as from the length of time they would take up, were they regularly continued. But the Dancing-masters enliven the entertainment by introducing between the minuets their High Dances, (which is a kind of Double Hornpipe) in the execution of which they excell perhaps the rest of the World. I wish I had it in my power to describe to you the variety of figures and steps they put into it. Besides all those common to the hornpipe, they have a number of their own, which I never before saw or heard of; and their neatness and quickness in the performance of them is incredible: so amazing is their agility, that an Irishman, who was standing by me the other night, could not help exclaiming in his surprise 'that 'by Jesus, he never saw children so *handy* 'with their *feet* in all his life.'

The motion of the feet is indeed the only thing that is considered in these dances, as they rather neglect than pay any attention to the other parts of the body; which is a great pity, since it would render the dance much more complete and agreeable, were the attitude of the hands and positions of the body more studied and understood by them. From the practice of these high dances one great advantage is derived to the young men, in giving prodigious powers to their ancles and legs: but I cannot say it is an ornamental advantage either to them or to the ladies; as it makes them too large in those parts for the proportion of the rest of the body, and takes off that fine tapering form which is so essential to real beauty.

I do not know any place in the world where dancing is made so necessary a part of polite education as in Edinburgh. For the number of inhabitants I suppose there are more Dancing-masters than in any other City; who gain large fortunes, though they instruct on very moderate terms, from the number of scholars who constantly attend them. In general they may be said to be very good ones, as well those of their own Country as Foreigners from most of the polite parts of Europe.

rope. Besides minuets and these high dances, they instruct the children in cotillons and allemandes, but not many of them, as they are sensible of their incapability of succeeding. In dancing, as in many other things, instruction and precept alone do not convey ideas so well as example and practice. Had they some few as excellent as Miss Lucinda B— to shew them what it was to move gracefully, elegantly, and unaffectedly, I do not doubt but that then they might make some progress, and reach some degree of perfection. I wish, therefore, for the benefit of this City, that you, and half a dozen of your female acquaintance, would pass the next winter in Edinburgh, in order to give them a model of a complete dancer.

Believe me, Dear Lucinda,
sincerely Yours.

LETTER

LETTER XLII.

On the Assemblies public and private.

To Miss Lucinda B——

Edinburgh, May 19, 1775.

DEAR LUCINDA,

YOUR description of the Festino afforded me no little amusement; and I think myself as fortunate in hearing your account of it, as you can do in being present at the reality. But there is one thing at which I cannot be a little angry; that you should entertain such a contemptible idea of our amusements: I say our, for I have been in this country so long, that I begin to think myself an inhabitant of it. Suffer me to inform you, that we too have Assemblies, brilliant as the eyes of Beauties can make them, with which this country abounds, and which every place of public resort in Edinburgh can boast of, if they had no other inducements or charms to recommend them.

I assure

I assure you the Assemblies afford a very agreeable diversion: they are governed by seven Directors and seven Directresses, one of whom manages the dancing alternately, and performs the part of Mistress of the Ceremonies. As the room is too small for the company who generally frequent them, it is impossible for all to dance at the same time: to prevent, therefore, the inconvenience and confusion which must necessarily be occasioned, the Lady Directress is obliged to divide the company into Sets, and suit them according to their rank and quality, putting about twelve couple in a Set. After this *etiquette* is over, the first Set dance minuets, beginning in the order of the tickets which are distributed by the Lady Directress, and then one country dance, in the middle of the room, which is surrounded by chairs, to prevent the rest of the company from interfering with the dancers. At the conclusion of this, the second Set begin, and then the third and fourth in their respective turns, till all the Sets have danced their minuet and country dance, and then the first begin again a country dance, and the other follow as at first.

This

This mode of conducting the Assemblies is much approved of by the inhabitants of this City, and certainly has many conveniencies; as you dance with the greatest ease, order, and regularity, from having the whole room, and no crowd or interruption; besides you generally know your company, which gives the public all the advantages of a private entertainment. But then the young Ladies, who are fond of dancing, complain, that by this means they are deprived of that pleasure, as it seldom happens that a Set can dance oftener than twice. Indeed the worst circumstance attending it is, that you are often prevented entirely from dancing, as there may be too many Sets for it ever to come to your turn; but for my own part, I think that the comfort with which you dance balances every disadvantage, and makes it, upon the whole, a most eligible form for an Assembly.

Were the Scotch Gentlemen disposed to gallantry, this manner of managing the Dancing, would afford them the finest opportunity they could wish, as they are left the whole evening to furnish entertainment
and

and converſation for their partners. But obſervations on the cloaths and dancing of the party who are performing, too often fill up the vacant interval; and, inſtead of ogling, ſighs, proteſtations, and endearments, the Lady ſits envying the more fortunate ſtars of her companion who is dancing, whilſt her partner yawns for the approaching period of his own exhibition.

Ever ſince I have been in Edinburgh, the office of Lady Directreſs has been diſcharged by Mrs. Murray, ſiſter to Lord Mansfield; who executes her part with ſo much ſucceſs, that the other Ladies fear to attempt it after her; and, indeed, ſhe deſerves every encomium that can be beſtowed on her. 'As long as Mrs. Murray obliges the Public with her aſſiſtance, the City of Edinburgh cannot wiſh 'for a more agreeable entertainment, than their Aſſemblies; but if any thing ſhould happen to deprive them of her abilities, it is imagined they would furniſh themſelves with a better room, where a different plan would be adopted.

How far it is better for a public amuſement to be under the influence of a Lady, or how far the Scotch Gentlemen are to be justified in giving so much trouble and fatigue to the fair sex, I will not pretend to say; but thus far I can speak from experience, that nothing was ever conducted with more propriety and regularity, than they are at present; nor was I ever at any Assembly where the authority of the Manager was so observed or respected. With the utmost politeness, affability, and good humour, Mrs. Murray attends to every one. All petitions are heard, and demands granted which appear reasonable.

The company is so much the more obliged to Mrs. Murray, as the task is by no means to be envied. The crowd which immediately surrounds her on her entering the room, the impetuous applications of *chaperons*, maiden-aunts, and the earnest intreaties of lovers to obtain a ticket in one of the first Sets for the dear object, render the fatigue of the office of Lady Directress almost intolerable; and I am sensible, few would undertake it, did not Mrs. Murray's zeal and endeavours meet with universal approbation.

Besides

Besides minuets and country-dances, they in general dance reels in separate parts of the room; which is a dance that every one is acquainted with, but none but a native of Scotland can execute in perfection. Their great agility, vivacity, and variety of horn-pipe steps, render it to them a most entertaining dance; but to a stranger, the sameness of the figure makes it trifling and insipid, though you are employed during the whole time of its operation; which, indeed, is the reason why it is so peculiarly adapted to the Scotch, who are little acquainted with the attitude of standing still.

Allemandes and Cotillons are neither admired nor known in public companies in this City. Those Ladies who have seen them danced in Paris or London, are unwilling to introduce them, well-knowing how little calculated they are for the meridian of their country.

I was lately at an Assembly here on the Queen's birth-day, where Mrs. Murray representing her Majesty, presided in the chair, and received the proper compliments. It was conducted with the usual elegance and propriety,

priety, and was so crowded, that not half the Sets could dance that wished to do it. I assure you I never saw a stronger appearance of loyalty even at St. James's, or more rejoicing on any public event.

But besides the general Assemblies, there are a number of private ones given by societies, clubs, or subscription, and every week is productive of something new. Among the rest, the matrons and married Ladies give an Assembly and Entertainment to the young Ladies, to whom they distribute tickets to provide themselves partners. You may be sure the old ones are not backward in their invitation. Each of them is squired by some antiquated beau, who, with his best cloaths, brushes up his best minuet, and revives in imagination the feats of ancient times.

In return for this Ball the Gentlemen of the Capilaire club give another equally elegant and polite, with a supper, ices, and every thing that luxury can invent. After the Ladies are withdrawn, the Gentlemen, in conformity with the manner of this Country, retire into a private room, where each sacrifices his
understanding

understanding and health to wishing, in full bumpers, the health of his fair partner; who, if she has any understanding, must ridicule, condemn, and abhor the custom. But the Scotch Gentlemen are so resolute in their determination, that many of them, immediately after the departure of the Ladies, retire for a short time, in order to change their dancing apparel, and put on a dress more adapted to the occasion of riot and excess.

Happy would it be for our sex, had every female that good sense, which you are possessed of! Was the conversation of all of them as agreeable, mankind would be so far from finding happiness in dissipation and wine, that a drunkard and a coward would be equally ignominious. The society of the women would afford them the only real pleasure; and, instead of remorse, instead of

"Thick-ey'd, musing, cursed melancholy,"

which pursue the votary of Bacchus, the debauchee, and the gamester, a constant serenity of mind, from the improvement of their knowledge, a chearful confidence from the conviction of reason and sound judgment; a uniform life and spirit in their conversation, would render them tender parents, affectionate friends, and faithful lovers.

My dear Lucinda,

   believe me sincerely yours.

LETTER XLIII.

On the Police of Edinburgh.

To R. D. Esq;

Edinburgh, May 25, 1775.

SIR,

AN Englishman, who has passed much of his life in London, and who has been entertained every morning with some dreadful account of Robbery or Outrage committed the evening before, would be much surprised, on coming into this City, to find that he might go with the same security at midnight as at noonday. A man, in the course of his whole life, shall not have the fortune here to meet with an house-breaker, or even so much as a single foot-pad: and a woman shall walk along the streets at any hour in an evening, without being " broke " in upon," as Tristram Shandy says, " by " one tender salutation." At eleven o'clock, all is quiet and silent; not so much as a watchman

watchman to disturb the general repose. Now and then at a late, or rather an early hour in the morning, you hear a little party at the taverns amusing themselves by breaking the bottles and glasses; but this is all in good humour, and what the constable has no business with.

As I do not imagine this is owing to the peculiar dispositions of the Scotch; for human nature, when occasion presents itself, is, I take it, the same in all places, we must attribute it to the excellence of the Police. The City Guard, who, I assure you, are very terrible looking men, and perform their exercise every day in the High-street, to shew people what they can do, have their stations, during the whole night, in the street, to prevent any quarrels or disorders that may arise there. These are relieved by others in their turn; so that the duty is performed by all of them in succession.

This Guard is of very old standing, and commanded at present by no less a person than the Provost of Edinburgh, who is generally a tradesman, and consequently much used to arms. But I can with great truth

truth inform you, that the command has been vested in persons equally formidable for two centuries or more. In the year 1580, the Common Council of Edinburgh formed citizens into companies of fifty men each, and appointed burgesses of the best experience in martial affairs to command them; for, as the Act wisely says, "It hath "been found by experience, in many coun- "tries, that it is not so much the multi- "tude that overcometh, as the experience "and skill of well-trained and exercised sol- "diers, seeing it is the knowledge of warfare "that emboldeneth to fight." So the experienced burgesses led on this bold band of citizens as often as their skill was called for. At present, however, their great knowledge in warfare has not many opportunities of shewing itself; and as they are chiefly used as a guard during the night time, their heroic deeds are unfortunately concealed from public view. To do them justice, however, they seldom sleep upon their post, which is saying a great deal for men who are not kept awake by the fear of an enemy. But whether the extreme good order and regularity which is obferved in the ftreets, and the very few robberies which are committed, are entirely owing to thefe military men or not, is rather difficult to determine. I believe there are other people of a more civil nature, who fhare with them the hardfhips as well as the honour of accomplifhing fo great a tafk. Thefe are a fet of men who are called in this country Cadies, and who have been formed many years into a fociety for their own emolument and the public good; a fociety which is probably as ufeful and extraordinary as ever exifted. To tell you what thefe people do is impoffible; for there is nothing almoft which they do not do. They are the only perfons who may truly be faid to have attained univerfal knowledge; for they know every thing and every body; they even know fometimes what you do better than you yourfelf. The moment a ftranger comes into Edinburgh, they know it: how long he is to ftay; whither he is going; where he comes from, and what he is. In regard

gard to the Police, this may be a convenience, otherwise it would be a great nusance. A certain number of them stand all day long, and most of the night, at the top of the High-street, waiting for employment. Whoever has occasion for them, has only to pronounce the word " Cadie," and they fly from all parts to attend the summons. Whatever person you may want, they know immediately where he is to be found. Trust them with what sum of money you please, you are quite safe: they are obliged by the rules of their Order to make good every thing they lose. A gentleman once sent one of these Mercuries with a letter inclosing bills for some hundred pounds; the man lost it, and the Society (who are responsible for these losses) restored the sum to the proprietor.

These men act likewise in the capacity of Sir John Fielding's Thief-takers in London, and take all the thieves here, as they have intelligence of the places where such a person is likely to be found. In short, nothing can escape them: and what Doctor Johnson says of a Frenchman may be truly applied to them;

"Each gainful trade a ſtarving Cadie knows,
"And bid him go to Hell—to Hell he goes."

Theſe are the people who are the great means of preſerving the public peace, and of preventing all thoſe crimes which are generally perpetrated under a Police which is ill-obſerved. It is the certainty of puniſhment which prevents guilt: for when a man is ſure of being diſcovered, he dreads the commiſſion of the ſmalleſt offences. It is well known that the frequency of aſſaſſination in many parts of Italy, is entirely owing to the ſanctuaries which protect the offenders. A man has only to calculate the diſtance he has to run, and the probability he has of being caught, and he perpetrates a murder with impunity.

Nothing can reflect more honour on this City, than the ſafety in which every man finds himſelf and his property. An Engliſhman, who has his houſe broken open twenty times in his life, calls it his Caſtle; and though

though he is afraid of stirring out of his doors after it is dark, he is continually boasting to you of his liberty, and the security of his person.

The Police of Paris has long been a subject of general and deserved admiration. A man may pass through the streets there at any hour in an evening, with as little danger as he would in the middle of the day.

It is by the same means as in Paris that the Police in Edinburgh is so well observed, which otherwise, from its populousness, and the style of the buildings, is as much calculated to conceal villains, as any city whatever. No people in the World undergo greater hardships, or live in a worse degree of wretchedness and poverty, than the lower classes here; but though they are very poor, I believe, as a nation, they are very honest; at least, their dishonesty takes a different turn, from that of the common people in England: it runs into that concealed line of acting which, under the mask of insinuation and hypocrisy, works its way gradually to the purpose it wishes to attain, and not into that open and avowed villainy

villainy which feeks a miferable and precarious fubfiftence at the hazard of life, and which, even in danger and death, difcovers a fortitude that ought to be the refult of virtue alone.

In defiance of the rigour of the penal laws in England; in fpite of the immenfe numbers who die by the executioner, I do not find that the laws are in the leaft better obferved, or fewer people robbed. From this confideration I am convinced that frequent executions are not of that utility many people think them of. " It has been obferved," fays Voltaire, " that " a man after he is hanged is good for no- " thing; and that punifhments invented for " the good of fociety, ought to be ufeful to " fociety: it is likewife evident, that a fcore " of ftout robbers condemned for life to " fome public work would ferve the ftate in " their punifhments, but that hanging them " is a benefit to nobody but the Execu- " tioner."

If the mildnefs of penal laws were an inducement to commit crimes, the Scotch would encourage more villains and robbers than any

Nation

Nation under the Sun, for they spare as many as they possibly can: but the contrary is very evident; and in all the robberies that ever happened, no act of wanton cruelty, or unnecessary offence has been known. The gaols here are likewise a convincing proof that the malefactors are neither so ingenious nor so hardened in villainy as with us.

In short, look where you will, you find that, under that numerous species of laws which form the police of every country, the mildest and most lenient are productive of the fewest crimes possible; and that good intelligence, with proper inspection, and not rigorous punishment, are the only true means of preserving public peace. Every man who passes any time in this Country will be convinced that too much cannot be said of the excellence of the Scotch laws in this respect, and the Magistrates who dispense them. The conviction that your person and property are really secure, is the truest argument of liberty in every nation; unless we agree with an old Commentator, that liberty is " *jus faciendi* " *quicquid velis*;" and that every body has a

right

right to do what they think proper:—a definition which moſt people ſeem inclined to give it: and which, as long as it continues in theory, may be very well—but Heaven defend us from the practice!

I have the honour to be, &c.

LETTER XLIV.

On the State of the Agriculture near Edinburgh.

To R. D. Efq;

SIR,

IN compliance with a former promife I will endeavour to give you fome fhort account of the country adjacent to Edinburgh, and the ftate of their Agriculture, though I cannot fay it deferves your attention. The three immenfe hills adjoining to the City, and which are named "Arthur's Seat," "Salifbury Craig," and "Charlton Hill," are fo broken, and in many parts fo precipitately fteep, that it is impoffible to ufe them in tillage, and they are therefore always kept in grafs, and fed upon by fheep, cows, &c. On the fummit of thefe hills the inhabitants of Edinburgh play at their favourite game of *Golf*; and the poffeffors of the ground turn it to better account by letting part of it for that purpose, than by grazing the whole of it. Around the edges of Charlton Hill they are now cutting out a walk, which, from the amazing height of the hill, and the variety of the prospects, will, when it is entirely finished, be one of the most extraordinary ones in Europe.

The Plough made use of in the Lowlands is that without wheels, which they draw with one or two horses, as the soil is very light and shallow. The ground all around the Town is pasture, and rented by the inhabitants of the City for their cattle; and they pay for it, upon an average, the sum of three pounds *per* Acre. Of Corn land the quantity is very inconsiderable, and the crops are in general very bad. In some measure this may be attributed to the poorness of the land; but the Scotch are by no means good farmers. Agriculture is one of those things of which they seem to have but a very indifferent idea, and which the learned here have never thought of studying. Their fortunes in general consist either of ready money

or

or of houses in Edinburgh; for those who possess landed property have it in the Highlands, which are almost incapable of cultivation. There are in this Country very few of that middle class of Gentry, as with us, who reside upon their own estates, and who, unambitious of mixing with the World, are contented with taking care of their own lands, and living by their industry; and who think themselves no inconsiderable members of society, while confined to the narrow limits of their own *demesnes*; and while they are improving their hereditary income, add to the beauty of their country, and to Agriculture in general.

I believe many of the Scotch think this study below their regard. How shocking would such sentiments be held in England! where of late years Agriculture has been matter of universal consideration, and men of the first abilities and most elevated rank have been ambitious of shining in the characters of Farmers; and shunning all the more brilliant scenes of public life, where real genius ought to to be exerted, have retired without honour, and been satisfied with obscurity.

Nay, so far has this fashion been carried, that a * Gentleman shall travel into a remote country, the language of which he does not understand, and looking out of his chaise window as he passes along, shall think it necessary, on his return, to publish a long and tedious account of the Husbandry of every country he has seen.

Some years ago every man who travelled went in the character of a Builder, taking the measure of this dome, and that temple, and then relating to his countrymen the height, circumference, &c. of each: now every person acts the part of a Farmer; he enquires after the crops, turns over the soil, and tastes the manure, for the benefit of his countrymen, who are to be entertained with his discoveries.

Poor Yorick laughed the first of these fooleries out of countenance; we now find

---

* Vide Mr. Marshal's Tour through Sweden, Russia, &c. and which is filled with these Remarks.

the want of his talents to ridicule the second: but alas! " where are his gibes and " his merriment now?"—all paſſed away and forgotten with himſelf!

I have the honour to be, &c.

LETTER XLV.

On the Scotch Music.

To R. L. T. Esq.

Edinburgh, May 27, 1775.

DEAR SIR,

AMONGST the other polite arts which are encouraged and admired in this Country, Music seems to have as many votaries, and to be esteemed as much, as any other. There are few places where it is made a more requisite part of female education than at Edinburgh: almost every one above the common rank of mankind have some knowledge and taste in it. Though many of the tunes which in England are styled Scotch airs, are the production of modern imitators, and have been forged on the World as the genuine composition of this Country, when they have been the offspring of a London Music-shop; yet there are some of very great antiquity, which afford a specimen

cimen of the genius of the inhabitants in former ages in this science, and which to this day are universally approved of, as expressing the natural feelings of the heart, in the most tender, sympathetic, and soothing style. As every one of these pieces that have been handed down to us are of vocal music, it is most probable that the words, which are often highly poetical and beautiful, have been the cause of their longævity; notwithstanding as musical literature, they are greatly meritorious, and perhaps of the most emphatic, plaintive, sentimental harmony, of any compositions that ever existed.

Of the originality of this music, and of its estimation in foreign countries as well as in this, there cannot be a greater proof than an anecdote from Tassoni, the author of the celebrated Mock-heroic Poem of Sechia rapita, who, in his Pensieri diversi, tells us in what esteem a kind of music which was peculiar to this nation, was held even in Italy, that seat of the Muses, long before the time of David Rizzio; and by his description of it, exactly characterizes that species of which even now we have many and delightful examples *.

As the excellency of vocal music consists in the harmony being adapted to the sense and pronunciation of the words, as likewise to the accent and cadence of the language it is set to, which are different in every different country, and vary as much as the genius and disposition of the inhabitants; so these ancient Scotch tunes are wonderfully beautiful in this respect, and appear with more charms in proportion as you become acquainted with the natives, and their manner of speaking and expressing their thoughts; as they are

---

* It is generally imagined, that David Rizzio was the Author of this species of Music: but if credit may be given to Tassoni, it is of much greater antiquity; whose words are,

"Noi ancora possiamo connumerar trà Nostri Jacobo Re di Scozia, che non pur Cose sacre compose in Canto, ma trovó da sestesso una nuova Musica lamentavole & mesta, differente da tutte l'altre. Nelche poi è stato imitato da Don Carlo Gesvaldo Principe di Venosa, chi in questa nostra Età hà illustrata anch' Egli la Musica con nuove mirabile invenzione."

formed

formed on founds which are familiar to you every where in the country, and here alone have their peculiar grace. Were you to hear a Scotch lady repeat the verses of any of the true original songs, and afterwards to sing them to the notes, you would find such an affinity to the tone of her voice in speaking, that the notes would appear only the accents of the language made exquisitely sweet and musical. The sentiments also of these songs consisting of that pensive, dying softness, and expressed in such tender and passionate words, which are so conformable to the genius and inclination of the women, whose hearts are susceptible of every impression when assisted with the power of such harmony, make it impossible to conceive any human eloquence more delightful and more persuasive.

The modern Music of this Country (of which there are very few Composers, notwithstanding the great encouragement it meets with, and makes one of the principal diversions of every great town in Scotland) is not of the same excellence, or breathes that natural spirit and agreeable sweetness which distinguishes that of former times. At present they rather endeavour to imitate other nations, than to have a style peculiar to themselves; and their pieces are made up of such variety of tastes, that they may be said to be harmonic Oglios. Such is the case of my Lord Kelly, whose admirable talents and genius in this science have been corrupted and restrained by his poorly copying the compositions of other masters. Had he pursued that originality of fancy and expression, which is really natural to him, there is no doubt but that Scotland, at this hour, might have boasted her musical excellence, equal to any other nation in Europe. As a proof of this, I refer you to those wilder compositions, where his proper genius has broke forth, where his imagination heated by wine, and his mind unfettered by precept, and unbiassed by example, has indulged itself in all its native freedom. But, in general, too close an observance of the Italian manner has corrupted him, and many other composers of this Country; and, I am afraid, is spreading also its contagion in ours. In a few years, probably,

we

we shall have no more remains of the true English Music, than there is here at present of that charming species which I before mentioned, and which, if beauty could insure immortality, ought never to die.

I would not have you imagine, from what I have said, that I am not an admirer of Italian Music; so far from it, I greatly esteem it, and think it deserves the highest degree of commendation as Italian Music, as Music adapted to the spirit and disposition of Italy; in which sense it certainly excells the music of all other countries, which are less suited to the sentiments and expression of their respective inhabitants. But this is so far from being the reason why other nations should imitate it, that it is the very reason they should not. It is the same with music as with languages: the tone and pronunciation of which express the sentiments of any particular people, much better than the same words delivered by the mouth of a foreigner; as likewise words of quite an opposite signification, are often expressed in different languages in the same tone of voice. Thus, for instance, sentences of

interrogation

interrogation and admiration, by an Italian, would be spoken in tones not unlike the ordinary tones of the English voice when we are angry. That musical expression varies in the same manner, you will stand in need of no other demonstration than to translate any foreign song into our tongue; so that the same note serves the corresponding word in each, and you will see, provided you have a perfect knowledge of the harmony of both languages, what different ideas will be excited by it, accordingly as it is applied to words; and how improperly, perhaps, it would express the passion in the English.

One of the principal entertainments in Edinburgh is a Concert, which is supported by subscription, and under the direction of a Governor, deputy Governor, Treasurer, and five Directors, who procure some of the best performers from other countries, and have a weekly Concert in an elegant room, which they have built for that purpose, and which is styled St. Cecilia's Hall. It is rather too confined; but in every other respect the best accommodated to Music of

any

any room I ever was in. The figure of it is elliptical, and the roof is vaulted, and a single instrument is heard in it with the greatest possible advantage. The Managers of the Concert have a certain number of tickets to distribute to their friends, so that none are admitted but the people of fashion. Though the band is a good one in general, yet I cannot say much in favour of the vocal performers.

The natives of this country are not remarkable for their abilities in singing; and except in a few of the real Scotch tunes, I have never met with a voice that had either compass or an agreeable tone. But in order to make up this deficiency in their own countrymen, the managers take care to have some of the best singers from London and Italy. At present they have some tolerably good ones, who are not quite so admired as a Gabrielli or a Tenducci would be: the latter of whom, before he fled from Great Britain, resided here a considerable time, and was one cause of introducing that rage for Italian music, which is now so predominant. Indeed,

the

the degree of attachment which is shewn to Music in general in this country, exceeds belief. It is not only the principal entertainment, but the constant topic of every conversation; and it is necessary not only to be a lover of it, but to be possessed of a knowledge of the science to make yourself agreeable to society.

In vain may a man of letters, whose want of natural faculties has prevented him from understanding an art, from which he could derive no pleasure, endeavour to introduce other matters of discourse, however entertaining in their nature: every thing must give place to music. Music alone engrosses every idea. In religion a Scotchman is grave and abstracted; in politics serious and deliberate: it is in the power of harmony alone to make him an enthusiast.

What a misfortune it is to the country, and how trifling does it appear to a stranger, to find so many philosophers, professors of science, and respectable characters, disputing on the merits of an Italian fiddle, and the precisenes of a demiquaver; while
poetry,

poetry, painting, architecture, and theatrical amusements, whose province it is to instruct as well as to amuse, here couch beneath the dominion of an air or a ballad, which at best were only invented to pass away a vacant hour, or ease the mind from more important duties!

I have the honour to be

yours sincerely.

LETTER

LETTER XLVI.

To R. D. Esq.

SIR,

YOU have already received so many letters from this country, that you will imagine I think of making it my residence; and, in truth, I have in some measure begun to consider it as my home. But alas! every thing in this vile world is transitory and uncertain. After all the agreeable hours I have passed here, the remembrance of which will ever be dear to me, I am on the point of taking my leave of this kingdom. Travellers, you know, generally affect a sorrow on parting with those who have received them civilly; and sometimes, probably, may feel one. But I can assure you, that on this occasion it is not necessary " to assume a virtue which I have not." I am so well convinced of the merit of those I leave behind me, that I feel the most sincere regret for my departure.

The

The wandering life I have hitherto led, has by no means extinguished these sensations: for, though I despise all attachments to this place or the other, merely for being such, I make it my study to conform, as far as I can, to the opinions, and even to the prejudices of every country into which I go. Every man should do so, because it is the means of making his own happiness.

Whatever you may think of the disagreeableness of hurrying from place to place, unsettled and unconnected, let me tell you, that travelling has its pleasures. Solon, you will remember, was so well convinced of the truth of this maxim, that he began his travels at fifty years of age. The celebrated Madame Bocage says, " notwithstanding the
" regret of leaving our friends, the time
" spent in travelling is probably the most
" pleasing of our lives, and that which
" passes away most rapidly. By habit, ob-
" jects become insipid to us, as we do to
" others. Let us then change our country
" and we shall become new: for, though
" mankind are the same every where, their
" passions and their manners, which we
" observe

"observe under different forms, continually excite our wonder, and furnish new matter for our attention."

But it is not the present moment alone that is thus profitably or pleasingly employed; it is the recollection of these scenes in future life. A man should not forget that there are a number of solitary years in reversion, when the body, weakened by sickness or worn out by pain, forcibly tied down to one place, leaves the mind free and active, and whose reflections must then be his only entertainment. If he has none of these resources in his own mind, his situation is truly pitiable: for the season of the passions is of very short duration.

But adieu to moralizing! The little time I have now left me, must be employed in acknowledging the numerous civilities I have received, and in parting from those I most esteem. I wish this last office over, for it is a very painful one, and answers no one purpose that I know of, but that of making us more melancholy. Were I to spare my own feelings alone on this occasion, I might probably be willing to escape without the

the ceremonies of an audience; but the gratitude I owe the Scotch, must make me forego such a thought. The last impressions we make, too often stamp the character; and as you have already seen the favourable opinion I entertain of this nation, I should be happy to find myself, in my turn, not entirely disregarded or forgotten. But be those sentiments what they may, on my part I shall have fulfilled my wishes, if I have divested you of those prejudices which too many English indulge in regard to the Scotch, and convinced you that the Inhabitants deserve our attention not less than the country itself.

I have the honour to be, &c.

FINIS.

www.ingramcontent.com/pod-product-compliance
Lightning Source LLC
Chambersburg PA
CBHW030428300426
44112CB00009B/898